Arbitrary Lines

Arbitrary Lines

How Zoning Broke the American City and How to Fix It

M. Nolan Gray

ISLANDPRESS | Washington | Covelo

Library of Congress Control Number: 2021951324

All Island Press books are printed on environmentally responsible materials.

Manufactured in the United States of America
10 9 8 7 6 5 4 3

Keywords: accessory dwelling unit (ADU); affordable housing; automobile dependency; commercial use; deed restriction; density; Houston, Texas; industrial use; land use regulation; minimum lot size; parking requirement; residential use; segregation; sprawl; sustainability; Yes In My Backyard (YIMBY)

*For Mom and Dad—
who moved to a city and
made it all possible.*

Contents

Part II

Part III

Introduction

As Americans, we take comfort in the idea that we have the right to plan our own lives. We are unique in our confidence that it is within our power to move to a better life, as so many of our ancestors did. Where other countries talk about managing stagnation and even decline, we stand undaunted in our assurance that the limits of our wealth and the frontier of innovation lay well into the future. Liberated from Old World hierarchies, we Americans fancy our home a place where any person, regardless of their color, creed, or class background, can improve their lot. And if there are broader forces that threaten our way of life, so much the worse for them; progress, and the change it brings, is intrinsic to who we are.

The idea that a stodgy rule book could set the terms of our lives from on high is fundamentally at odds with our national ethos. And yet, such is the state of America under zoning. From unremarkable origins, the arbitrary lines on zoning maps across the country have come to dictate where Americans may live and work, forcing cities into a pattern of growth that is segregated and sprawling. Once the exclusive domain of local planners, concurrent crises surrounding housing costs, underwhelming economic growth, racial and economic inequality, and climate change have thrust zoning into the public consciousness. Now more than ever, there is an appetite for reform. Yet we can do better: it's time for America to move beyond zoning.

At surface level, zoning is an impossibly boring topic, even by the terms of public policy debate. The mere thought of a weeknight zoning hearing or a seven-hundred-page zoning ordinance is enough to make even the most enthusiastic policy wonk's eyes glaze over. Until recently, zoning might have been blithely dismissed as a mere technical matter, simply a way of rationalizing our cities, a planning policy so obvious as to be beyond reproach.

But zoning is at once so much less and so much more. While occasionally used as a stand-in for city planning or building regulations more broadly, its scope is far more limited: at a basic level, all zoning does is segregate land uses and regulate densities. Your local zoning ordinance sets out various districts, each with detailed land-use and density rules, while an associated local zoning map establishes where these rules apply. The bread and butter of what most people think of as city planning—such as streets planning or building regulations—has almost nothing to do with zoning.

Yet from these seemingly innocuous zoning rules have emerged a set of endlessly detailed parameters controlling virtually every facet of American life. Arbitrary lines on zoning maps determine where you can live, by way of allowing housing to be built here but not there. Through a dizzying array of confusing and pseudoscientific rules, from "floor area ratio" restrictions to setback mandates, zoning serves to heavily restrict the amount of housing that may be built in any given neighborhood and the form it may take. In most major cities, zoning restricts roughly three-quarters of the city to low-slung single-family housing, banning apartments altogether.

The combined effect is that, in already built-out cities, zoning makes it prohibitively difficult to build more housing. As a result of the further tightening of zoning restrictions beginning in the 1970s, median housing prices have dramatically outpaced median incomes in many parts of the country over the past half century, such that millions of Americans now struggle to make rent or pay their mortgage each month. That is, if they have the luxury of having a stable home at all: in places where demand for new housing is especially high—as in cities like New York and Los Angeles—zoning restrictions have facilitated acute housing shortages, with attendant surges in displacement and homelessness. The COVID-19 pandemic has only expedited these trends, with home prices in 2020 rising at the fastest rate since 1979.[1]

The arbitrary restrictions that zoning places on cities also show up in our capacity to grow and innovate as a nation. By severely limiting new housing production in a handful of our most productive cities—including San Jose and Boston—we have made moving to our most prosperous regions a dubious proposition. Your income might double if you were to move from Orlando to San Francisco, but your housing costs would quadruple. Should we be surprised that many people are turning down that deal? For the first time in history, Americans are systematically moving from high-productivity cities to low-productivity cities, in no small part because these are the only places where zoning allows housing to be built. According to the 2020 Census, the population of California—one of our most productive and innovative states—is now basically stagnant, such that the Golden State will be losing a congressional seat for the first time in its 170-year history.

The downstream economic implications of this unprecedented reversal of historic trends are hard to overstate. After all, big cities make us more productive, in that they allow us to find a job perfectly suited to our talents and exchange ideas with colleagues working on the same issues. They provide a platform for individuals to experiment and innovate, nursing the young firms that go on to remake the American economy every few decades. To the extent that zoning has made it exponentially more difficult for Americans to move to these hubs of activity—for a software engineer to relocate to San Jose, or for a medical researcher to relocate to Boston—we are all poorer as a result.

Even beyond so-called "superstar cities," zoning shapes American life in many subtle but nefarious ways. As the Black Lives Matter movement has thrown into stark relief, America still has a long way to go in providing equal opportunity for all. And yet, few American cities recognize the fact that their zoning codes were drafted with the express intention of instituting strict racial and economic segregation. To this day, "the wrong side of the tracks" is not merely a saying but a place that is written into law as a zoning district drawn on a zoning map. To the extent that zoning can prohibit apartments in this neighborhood, or require homes to sit on a half-acre lot in that suburb, zoning is perhaps the most successful segregation mechanism ever devised.

This state of affairs is as true in the conservative suburbs of southern cities like Nashville and Atlanta as it is in progressive midwestern college towns like Ann Arbor and Madison. Tucked away behind a veil of "protecting community character," zoning has been used to determine who gets to live where since its inception. In practice, this has been used toward the end of rigid economic segregation, which in the American context often means racial segregation. In virtually every suburb in America, zoning maintains a kind of technocratic apartheid, preserving those areas most suitable to housing for the wealthy while locking less privileged Americans into neglected areas far from good jobs and quality public services.

Similarly, zoning makes more environmentally friendly forms of urban growth effectively illegal. By banning developers from building up, zoning forces them to build out. In the 2020s as in the 1950s, the lion's share of American housing growth continues to occur out on the edge of town, gobbling up farmland and natural areas that might otherwise have remained unbuilt. Despite burgeoning demand among a cross-section of Americans for apartments and townhouses closer to job centers, zoning locks cities into an urban design pattern—single-family homes sitting on vast lawns—that increasingly doesn't make environmental sense. Smaller homes with a shared wall can dramatically reduce residential energy consumption, and thus emissions, yet this is the precisely the type of housing that zoning makes most difficult to build.

At the same time, zoning assumes universal car-ownership, and all the emissions and traffic violence this entails. It does so by strictly segregating uses—no more corner groceries in neighborhoods—and forcing developers to build giant parking garages even in contexts where most residents or employees might prefer to bicycle or take the train. If you have ever wondered why more Americans don't walk or ride buses to work, as in most other developed countries, the simple answer is that it's illegal. In most American cities, zoning prohibits the densities needed to support regular bus service, let alone light-rail. The type of walkable, mixed-use, reasonably dense development patterns that might help to ameliorate climate change—patterns that prevailed before the twentieth century—are outright prohibited under most American zoning codes.

The good news is that it doesn't have to be this way. Reform is in the air, with cities and states across the country critically reevaluating zoning. In cities as diverse as Minneapolis, Fayetteville, and Hartford, the key pillars of zoning are under fire, with apartment bans being scrapped, minimum lot sizes dropping, and off-street parking requirements disappearing altogether.[2] Misbehaving suburbs find themselves under increasingly strict state scrutiny, with tighter rules requiring that each municipality allow its fair share of housing. More broadly, American urbanists are looking abroad for alternative ways to regulate land, including Japan's liberal approach to zoning.

But we can do better than small reforms. After all, zoning isn't merely a good policy misapplied toward selfish ends. Zoning is a fundamentally flawed policy that deserves to be abolished. Set aside for a moment the debilitating local housing shortages, the stunted growth and innovation, the persistent racial and economic segregation, and the ever-expanding sprawl: the very concept of zoning—the idea that state planners can rationally separate land uses and efficiently allocate density—has repeatedly failed to materialize. Far from the fantastical device imagined by early twentieth-century planners, zoning today has little to do with managing traditional externalities and works largely untethered from any guiding comprehensive plan.

It's high time we accept the need for zoning abolition and start thinking about what comes next. Happily, zoning is hardly the final word on managing urban growth. Cities found ways to separate noxious uses and manage growth for thousands of years before the arrival of zoning, and they can do the same after zoning. Indeed, some American cities—including Houston, America's fourth-largest city—already make land-use planning work without zoning. To the extent that zoning has failed to address even our most basic concerns about urban growth over the past century, it's incumbent on our generation to rekindle this lost wisdom and undertake the project of building out a new way of planning the American city.

This book lays the groundwork for this ambitious cause in three parts: Part I provides a clear explanation of what zoning is and where it comes from, clearing up common confusions and myths about how American cities regulate growth.[3] Part II examines four contemporary critiques of zoning: its role in increasing housing costs, restricting growth in our most productive cities, institutionalizing racial and economic segregation, and mandating sprawl. To tie it all together, part III sets out some of the efforts currently under way to reform zoning, makes the case for zoning abolition, and charts out how land-use regulation might work in the post-zoning American city.

This book is hardly the final statement on any of these matters. A complete explanation of zoning and its role in city planning could (and does) fill many textbooks. This book focuses on four popular critiques of zoning, but it would have been easy to add chapters on its role in holding back urban design and architectural innovation, undermining property rights, or fostering corruption. And this book's discussion of current reforms is hardly comprehensive, to say nothing of the closing meditation on what city planning might look like in a post-zoning world.

In the interest of keeping this book accessible to a general audience—the minute details of subdivision regulation don't exactly make for beach reading—additional material can be found in the back of the book. The appendix dives more broadly into the nitty-gritty of how planning works in the US. Interested readers should read it at the end of part I. For more information on the various themes and issues covered in this book, see the recommended readings.

One of the most compelling features of the American experiment is the dogged belief that things can always be better, that we need not be beholden to inherited institutions or assumptions. As I argue here, this is especially true of the way we plan our cities. In this regard, negative though it may at first seem, the project of this book is fundamentally constructive: beyond merely arguing against the arbitrary lines that hold us back, this book is a reminder that a more affordable, prosperous, equitable, and sustainable America is possible. Will you be a part of that journey?

Part I

CHAPTER 1

Where Zoning Comes From

For many Americans, their singular experience with city planning is a little game called *SimCity*. First released in 1989 and developed by legendary game designer Will Wright, the game invites players to plan their own cities. More of a sandbox than a conventional game with points or levels, each new "round" of *SimCity* presents players with a virgin field, the power to map out streets and zoning, and the freedom to do whatever they like from there. Poor planning decisions are punished with blinking indicators and unsolicited advice from AI advisors; wise planning decisions are rewarded with happy simulated citizens and a growing city.

Throughout the game, zoning is *the* essential power in the player's arsenal, granting them the ability to plop residential subdivisions here or industrial parks there, all while keeping incompatible uses separate. Pursuant to a grand, long-term vision, they can coordinate density to reflect the available infrastructure, keeping the city running like a well-oiled machine. All of these zoning decisions unfold without the pesky intervention of local politics; there are no ornery community boards or

NIMBY (Not In My Backyard) litigants in *SimCity*. The player-as-zon-ing-tyrant acts alone, beneficently applying their technical expertise to advance the general welfare of their growing city.

As you might expect, *SimCity* leaves a lot to be desired from a real-ism perspective: zoning isn't really about separating incompatible uses or coordinating densities, and local interest groups completely drive the process. Yet it's telling as a Rorschach test for how we *think* cities work: without zoning, the thinking goes, cities wouldn't work. While we today take the comprehensive, top-down control of land uses and densities for granted, the truth is that zoning is quite new. For most of human history, land uses casually intermingled and densities were capped by technological constraints more so than regulatory fiat. Dis-putes were generally settled among neighbors, and only the most obnoxious uses were banished to discrete districts. Rules on heights and setbacks, where they existed at all, were a function of health and safety considerations.

In the late nineteenth century, technological advances would allow cities to grow up and out like never before. By 1920, America had become a majority-urban nation. It's in this context of intense change that the seeds of a peculiar institution called zoning began to take root. While the rise of noxious urban industries or mounting infrastructure pressures are often assumed to be the key motivators for adopting zon-ing, the reality is more complicated. In most cities, bothersome indus-tries and booming infrastructure demands were issues long before the first modern zoning code was adopted in 1916. Better yet, rules and agencies were already addressing these issues in many American cities by the time zoning came online. What did zoning add?

Far from merely sorting out incompatible neighbors or coordinating growth, zoning aspired to rationally restructure and reorganize cities around the needs and preferences of the elites of a particular time and place. Beyond merely managing pollution or rationally allocating densities, zoning was the product of a strange coalition of interests who broadly sought to enrich incumbent property owners, lock existing neighborhoods in amber, institutionalize segregation, and mandate a sprawling vision of growth. Its defining contribution was to enshrine the single-family house as the urban ideal, while casting apartments as mere "parasites" and corner groceries as threats to public welfare. Absurd and unsavory though these positions may read to modern eyes, these peculiar motivations continue to form the basis of zoning to this day.

The first American zoning codes came online in 1916, riding on a wave of elite support spanning from commercial landlords to affluent homeowners. While New York City's 1916 Zoning Resolution usually gets all the attention, Berkeley, California's 1916 districting ordinance is more interesting to the extent that it comes closer to what zoning would eventually become. From these codes, each partly a response to a building boom, partly a response to specific groups of unwanted immigrants—Chinese in Berkeley, Eastern European Jews in New York City—zoning would slowly spread before getting a massive boost from the federal government.

Beginning in the early 1920s, then Secretary of Commerce—and future president—Herbert Hoover would draft and aggressively promote model state enabling legislation to allow municipalities to adopt zoning. In 1926, the Supreme Court gave zoning its blessing in *Euclid v. Ambler*, launching a nationwide boom in zoning adoption. And in the postwar period, through a steady stream of carrots and sticks from the federal government, zoning finally spread to cover nearly every incorporated area of the country alongside the rapid, federally subsidized emergence of suburbia. Most local governments had quietly adopted zoning by the 1970s, at times as a condition for receiving coveted federal funding for transportation infrastructure, housing subsidies, or disaster recovery.

The history of zoning, like the institution itself, is messy—perhaps by design. But if you take nothing else from this chapter, remember this: the comprehensive use segregation and density controls envisioned by zoning are a relatively recent invention. Far from the *SimCity* fantasy of merely regulating noxious uses or rationalizing growth, zoning's purpose from the start has been to prop up incumbent property values, slow the growth of cities, segregate the United States based on race and class, and enforce an urban ideal of detached single-family housing. While occasionally characterized as a bottom-up movement, the system we have today was heavily shaped by elite preferences of yesteryear and spread with persistent support from the federal government.

Land Use before Zoning

As normal as the typical American city may seem today, it has about as little in common with historical cities as a pug has with a wolf. These differences are most pronounced when it comes to the way we segregate uses and restrict densities. Take land use. Historically, there was comparatively very little segregation by use within cities, with shops, apartments, workshops, and mansions commonly intermingling.[1] There was likewise little distinction between home and work, with many urban residents either working in, or immediately adjacent to, their homes.

The same is true of density. The principal regulator of density was historically technology. A lack of cars or transit meant that most people walked, setting physical limits on the ability of cities to expand outward. In practical terms, this meant cities had to be compact, with even the largest cities constrained to a one-and-a-half-mile radius, such that even an edge-dweller could reach the core by foot within thirty minutes. Before the rise of innovations like steel framing or the elevator, building up was similarly restricted by gravity. Beyond a half dozen or so stories, building taller became uneconomical, as the base would have to expand to bear the full weight of the added stories.

This isn't to say that there were no formal use or density restrictions before the rise of zoning. For starters, the common law offered certain mechanisms whereby neighbors could seek relief from bothersome uses. If a use came with unwanted negative externalities—such as noise, smells, or pollution—a neighbor could seek an injunction against it as a private nuisance. In many cases, such land-use conflicts were resolved without even going to court, with the mere threat of litigation forcing neighbors to find a mutually agreeable compromise.

For certain uses bound to irritate neighbors—such as brickyards or tanneries—many cities and towns explicitly barred them from city limits or segregated them to the edges of town on the basis that they would be a public nuisance anywhere else. Similar regulations would address building materials and heights on the basis of fire safety, and beginning in the second half of the nineteenth century, many cities would adopt increasingly stricter housing standards to address public health concerns. While highly imperfect, this system largely addressed the challenges posed by urban land uses and densities without requiring regimented land-use controls.

Beyond districting noxious uses, city planning more broadly also preceded the rise of zoning. Nearly every great civilization has imposed some form of city planning, from the street grids of ancient Rome to the caste segregation of Vedic India. In the American context, many major cities, beginning with Thomas Holme's grid plan for Philadelphia, had adopted master street plans. This effort to plan cities went up a notch in the 1890s, with the City Beautiful movement giving rise to monumental public spaces across the country.[2] Similar movements surrounding parks and sewer improvements meant that by the 1910s, robust city planning institutions were already forming in most cities.

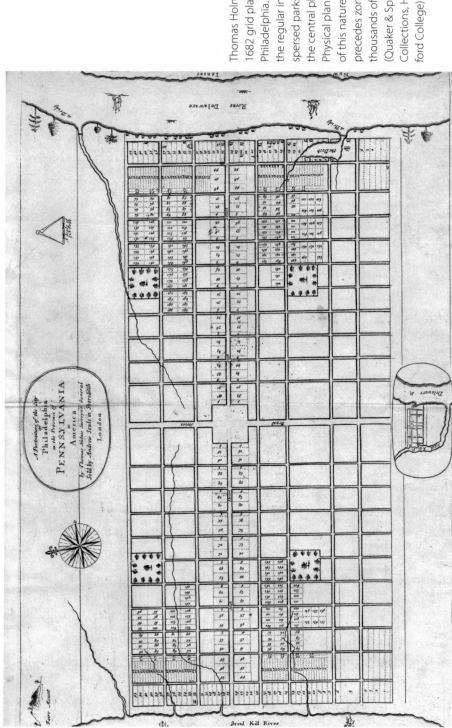

Thomas Holme's 1682 grid plan for Philadelphia. Note the regular interspersed parks and the central plaza. Physical planning of this nature precedes zoning by thousands of years. (Quaker & Special Collections, Haverford College)

What Changed?

By the 1940s, something had changed such that most major US cities had adopted a new and far more comprehensive set of land-use regulations: zoning. The noise and pollution associated with industrialization and the need to coordinate densities with public infrastructure improvements are often offered up in retrospect as the basis for modern zoning. Yet by the 1910s, neither issue was getting worse—indeed, after a century of trial and error, both were almost certainly getting better, with most American cities sporting sophisticated sewer and transit systems. What changed, such that a dramatic rethink of how we plan cities was seen as necessary?

In the late nineteenth century, major technological innovations removed traditional barriers to urban growth: innovations in building technology removed barriers to vertical expansion in the second half of the nineteenth century. With the first steel-frame building going up in Chicago in 1885, the physical constraints associated with load-bearing walls were removed, allowing structures to efficiently rise ten stories and above for the first time. Rapid improvements in elevator technology, such as Elisha Otis's safety locking mechanism, took the burden out of having an upper-floor office or warehouse. Collectively, these innovations allowed developers to build exponentially more floor area on the same plot of land, allowing densities to follow demand.[3]

All of this building supported ongoing urban industrialization between 1890 and 1920, leaving cities with a near insatiable appetite for labor. Between the mechanization of agriculture and this surging demand for industrial labor, mass migration from the countryside began, including among African Americans moving from the South as part of the Great Migration.[4] Concurrently, millions of immigrants flowed from southern and eastern Europe into northeastern and midwestern US cities, and to a lesser extent from East Asia into West Coast

The Home Insurance Building in Chicago, completed in 1885, is widely regarded as the first skyscraper for its use of a steel frame. The building was subsequently demolished and replaced with an even taller skyscraper in 1931. (Chicago Architectural Photographing Company, Library of Congress's National Digital Library Program)

cities. Cities such as Providence, Cleveland, and Los Angeles grew by a startling 50 percent or more between 1890 and 1920. This in turn triggered a boom in apartment construction, as demand for housing ballooned.

These innovations also gave rise to high-rise offices, supporting the agglomeration of major business districts and assembling the remarkable skylines that many American cities enjoy today. Never before was it easier to locate a firm in a central area, and never was it more important, as industrialization gave rise to a new class of big businesses with substantial office-space demands. While successive cycles of office building boom and bust were good for these commercial tenants, the steady supply of new office and industrial space kept rents low, creating uncertainty for landlords, who could see rents—and thus property values—plummet with the construction of a new skyscraper down the block. Thus, a constituency for comprehensive density restrictions that might temper this growth in major cities like New York City was born.

On the transportation front, the invention of the electric streetcar in the mid-1880s—and the rapid spread of new transit systems through roughly 1910—removed barriers to urban horizontal expansion. Often developed privately as part of a broader land development plan, streetcar lines soon stretched far outside cities and gave rise to streetcar suburbs, with apartments around stops gradually giving way to detached single-family homes.[5] The democratization of the car, beginning in 1908, shifted this suburbanization into overdrive.

The Anglo-American pastoral ideal of a detached single-family house surrounded by a yard dates back at least to Jefferson, with home life characterized by privacy and domesticity.[6] Yet when the modern American suburb first began to take shape in the post–Civil War period, it was largely restricted to the wealthiest by high transportation costs.[7] With a car, many middle-class households were no longer restrained to living within walking distance of work or transit, resulting in the rapid development of strictly low-density residential subdivisions at the edges of nearly every American city. Suburbia was no longer the exclusive domain of wealthy elites.

In the same way, cars released working-class households—and the apartments they inhabit—from downtown, while trucks released industry—and the warehouses it required—from needing to cluster around traditional transportation hubs like ports and rail depots. This gave both apartments and industry the opportunity to decamp for cheap land in the suburbs, threatening the strict class and use segregation that had historically characterized suburbs.[8]

One way of dealing with this problem, from the point of view of an affluent homeowner concerned with change, was through restrictive covenants. These covenants were in many ways a kind of proto-zoning, placing tight restrictions on land use and densities—no corner groceries, no subdividing homes into apartments. Their provisions would control issues like landscaping and architectural aesthetics, as well as prohibiting current owners from selling to certain disfavored racial and ethnic groups. These covenants were typically overseen and enforced by a neighborhood association, which would use the dues collected by residents to enforce their provisions. And in many contexts—particularly in new suburbs, where they could be applied as part of the initial development—covenants worked.

Yet covenants were highly imperfect as a mechanism of exclusion. For starters, they were virtually impossible to adopt in already built-out neighborhoods, requiring universal consent among property owners. Where they existed at all, they were occasionally unenforceable, owing to poor drafting or a pattern of nonenforcement, or came with set expiration dates. Even in the best of cases, covenants granted residents no control over nearby properties outside of their subdivision and forced them to pay for the enforcement of their own land-use preferences within their subdivision. These shortcomings threatened the "permanence" of elite suburban neighborhoods, to the dismay of affluent homeowners and the developers who hoped to sell to them. Thus, a constituency for comprehensive use segregation that might uphold segregation in the suburbs was born.[9]

1916

This confluence of factors came together at the crest of the Progressive Era, a wide-ranging movement to reform American society, covering everything from alcohol prohibition to antitrust regulation to eugenics to labor relations. With respect to cities, progressive reformers dreamed of replacing corrupt machine politics with scientific management by bureaucratic experts. Sometimes, it worked; sometimes, it didn't. The young city planning movement nonetheless latched on to zoning as a way to apply such a rational order to cities, with ambitions of resolving everything from slums to traffic congestion.

But in every political coalition, you need both a Baptist and a bootlegger.[10] The early zoning movement largely drew from, and found a key base of support among, upper-middle-class, Anglo-American property owners. Early Progressive promises of rationally planned cities quickly yielded to a basic pitch designed around this constituency: zoning will maintain your real estate investments, keep your neighborhood as it exists today, keep unwanted groups out of your community, and prioritize—above all else—the protection of your beloved detached single-family home.

This medley of promises manifested itself in different ways to suit different planning contexts as the first zoning ordinances started to come online in 1916. In New York City, the principal constituency was commercial landlords. The Fifth Avenue Association, which represented posh retail landlords, emerged as a key supporter of use segregation, as a way of preventing the creep of loft manufacturing toward the corridor. The issue was not so much any traditional externalities as it was the people that manufacturing brought into the neighborhood: on their lunch breaks, young, Jewish, immigrant workers would leave their factory floors to window-shop along Fifth Avenue. Retail landlords, characterizing these workers as "flies," feared they would scare off their elite clientele and so turned to zoning to shoo away their employers.[11]

Downtown in the Financial District, density controls found a slightly different constituency in office landlords. The Equitable Building, a vanity project of industrialist T. Coleman du Pont, had just been completed in 1915. Conventional wisdom holds that the building was shocking because of its massing, rising forty-two stories above an entire block without setbacks. Yet the Financial District already had skyscrapers, to say nothing of bulky buildings. What was exceptional about the Equitable Building was its density, flooding the Lower Manhattan office market with well over a million square feet of additional floor space, resulting in rising vacancies and falling rents.[12]

The resulting code, overseen principally by Edward Bassett—who would come to be known as the Father of American Zoning for his later advocacy—combined these desires for comprehensive use and density controls, resulting in a zoning ordinance that broke New York City out into use, height, and area districts.[13] For use segregation, the code employed a hierarchical framework dividing land uses by residential, business, and unrestricted districts. The code also assigned every city block to height districts, with heights capped at a multiple of adjacent street width. Above this height limit, buildings could rise alongside predetermined setbacks, producing New York's iconic ziggurat skyscraper pattern. Area districts likewise specified standards for yards and open spaces.[14]

By today's standards, New York's 1916 zoning code is surprisingly liberal. Modern zoning mainstays, like use subcategories or explicit floor area limits, are absent.[15] This is because the framers of New York's zoning ordinance saw themselves as balancing a desire for some control against a natural skepticism of this new institution. After all, as a historically unprecedented curtailment of property rights, the constitutionality of zoning was still very much in question, and one ill-conceived regulation risked a court decision that could imperil the entire project.[16] The strategy of starting small worked, and the code survived, expanding from just a small pamphlet to hundreds of pages over the coming decades, before the 1961 rewrite.

In the same year, seven other cities adopted zoning to much less fanfare. To the extent that Berkeley's 1916 ordinance more closely

In 1922, architect Hugh Ferriss produced a series of illustrations depicting the maximum permitted massing pursuant to New York City's 1916 zoning code.

Drawing, Study for Maximum Mass Permitted by the 1916 New York Zoning Law, Stage 4, New York City, 1922, Hugh Ferriss.

Drawing, Study for Maximum Mass Permitted by the 1916 New York Zoning Law, Stage 1, New York City, 1922, Hugh Ferriss.

Drawing, Study for Maximum Mass Permitted by the 1916 New York Zoning Law, Stage 2, New York City, 1922, Hugh Ferriss.

approximates a modern zoning code, and tracks onto the broader suburban movement to adopt zoning, it deserves a larger place in this story.
Where New York was a well-established city, Berkeley was a young suburb facing growth pressures for the first time. Between 1900 and 1920
alone, the city more than quadrupled in population, jumping from
13,214 to 56,036 residents. The rules adopted here would help to set
the terms of American suburban development and would play a key
role in defining America's explosive postwar growth.

In contrast to New York, where commercial landlords drove the movement for zoning, Berkeley's homeowners and industrial interests were
the main proponents behind modern zoning's West Coast debut. Demand
for zoning in Berkeley came principally from homeowners in the town's
affluent eastern residential sections and the builders who built for
them.[17] Restrictive covenants in the upscale neighborhood of Elmwood
had recently lapsed, and other neighborhoods were at similar risk.

But at risk of what, exactly? Pro-zoning materials at the time repeatedly point to the risk of apartments and industry entering low-density
residential neighborhoods.[18] Toward this end, the Berkeley ordinance
introduced the first single-family zoning district in the United States.[19]
Where most other early zoning ordinances defined broad residential
zones, agnostic as to whether they were filled with single-family homes
or apartments, Berkeley would be the first city to ban apartments in
areas otherwise deemed suitable for residential use.[20] By banning all but
the most expensive forms of housing—namely detached single-family
homes on large lots—Berkeley thus pioneered a form of state-sanctioned
residential class segregation that defines zoning to this day.

If the exclusionary intent of prohibiting apartments in wealthy neighborhoods is obvious, the desire to exclude industry from residential
neighborhoods might seem less objectionable. Yet when specific examples of undesirable industries are offered, the example is invariably of
Chinese-owned laundries, suggesting a similarly exclusionary intent.

While laundries historically could pose fire risks, the risk offered by Charles Henry Cheney, a key framer of Berkeley's 1916 zoning ordinance, is that they bring in "negroes and Orientals."[21] Indeed, the Berkeley city attorney separately characterized Berkeley's zoning proposal as part of a broader California tradition of segregating away "heathen Chinese."[22]

In addition to single-family homeowners, the other key constituency for zoning Berkeley was—curiously enough—industrial interests. As planning scholar Sonia Hirt observes, the strong support of the Manufacturers Association was indispensable in the push for zoning in Berkeley.[23] Where most zoning boosters promoted the institution as a way to keep industry out, the association's leadership characterized zoning as indispensable to *attracting* industry, with all the jobs and tax revenue it could bring.[24]

But what exactly was stopping industry from coming to Berkeley without zoning? As with fears about industry in residential neighborhoods, it wasn't an issue of health and safety, or even prudent planning. The issue was that people already lived among what industry leaders viewed as prime industrial districts, and these existing residents were well positioned to bring legitimate claims against bothersome new industrial developments that might try to enter the area. If zoning could be used to identify neighborhoods as "industrial," it could be used to clear a path for industrialization in areas otherwise desirable for other uses.

To accomplish this, the Berkeley zoning code introduced another important concept to zoning. Where other early codes adopted hierarchical zoning, allowing less intense uses into districts that allow more intense uses—that is to say, houses are allowed in factory districts, but not the other way around—Berkeley introduced flat zoning, which restricted each district to its designated use—no houses in industrial districts, no industry in residential districts.[25] By making this change, industrial zoning in Berkeley would not only insulate industries from complaints by existing residents but also block the entry of future residents, effectively reserving large swathes of town for industrial interests. Thus, the city's two key elite constituencies were fully bought into zoning.

Different though they may be, the origins of zoning in New York and Berkeley share one feature in common: the supposed planning function of zoning was secondary to the needs of special interests. Neither city had adopted a comprehensive plan prior to the adoption of zoning—new use and density standards were, at best, informed by elite norms and heuristics. In Berkeley, districts only took force after a petition from local property owners, which invariably involved wealthy residential neighborhoods attempting to throw up barriers to entry.[26] And New York City infamously lacks a comprehensive plan to this day. While subsequent efforts have tried to reverse this backward relationship between planning and zoning, to varying degrees of success, appreciating this early irony is key to understanding the true purposes of zoning.

The Federal Push

At the end of 1916, 8 municipalities had adopted some form of zoning, and over the next seven years, a steady stream of municipalities would follow, such that by 1923, 218 municipalities had adopted zoning.[27] On different stages, with different actors, the story of zoning adoption would be reenacted, with homeowners, industrialists, or commercial landlords playing the leading role as local political circumstances may require. Beginning in the 1920s, this stream would turn into a tidal wave, such that by 1936, well over 1,000 municipalities had adopted zoning. What happened?

The simple answer is that, in addition to its support among local elites, zoning found valuable friends in the federal government, particularly Herbert Hoover. Before going down as the president who stumbled into the Great Depression, Hoover was an energetic secretary of commerce under presidents Warren Harding and Calvin Coolidge. If issues like property values and segregation moved local reformers, Hoover was moved by an urban ideal of mass ownership of detached single-family houses, both to restore the "national character" and to stimulate the building industry.[28] As part of a sweeping push to standardize everything from housing finance to building materials, Hoover convened the Advisory Committee on City Planning and Zoning.[29]

Tasked with developing a model zoning statute, the committee was a who's who of the American city planning movement, with architect Frederick Law Olmsted Jr. and housing reformer Lawrence Veiller counted among its members. But from the start, it was Bassett—the man behind New York's 1916 ordinance—who was in the driver's seat. Where many committee members hoped to focus on the content of planning, Bassett brought a lawyer's eye to the work, focusing relentlessly on zoning process in a bid to build out a model zoning ordinance that could withstand court challenges.

The result was the Standard Zoning Enabling Act (SZEA), model legislation that states could adopt and in turn allow municipalities to adopt a local zoning ordinance.[30] Across nine heavily footnoted sections, the act sets out the basic processes of zoning, which hold to this day—more on this in the next chapter. The act says almost nothing about the *content* of the potential zoning regulations, pursuant to Bassett's goals of avoiding court challenges and providing local governments with maximum flexibility. While SZEA sets out a purpose for zoning, it does so in anodyne terms that bear little resemblance to the on-the-ground justifications for zoning, offering up unobjectionable goals such as preserving health and safety or reducing congestion. Little provision is made for regular updates to the ordinance, and city planning more broadly remains optional; little recognition is given to the actual motivations moving local reformers.

First released to state legislatures in draft form in 1922, SZEA would be an immediate hit. The committee subsequently published and widely distributed associated promotional materials, such as *Zoning Primer*, with the goal of popularizing zoning among industry groups. As Hoover brags in a preface to the final 1926 draft, in September 1921, only 48 municipalities had adopted zoning.[31] By the end of 1923, one year after SZEA's initial release, the number of municipalities that had adopted zoning had more than quadrupled. By 1936, after nearly two decades of relentless federal promotion, approximately 1,322 municipalities had adopted zoning.[32]

As it turns out, Bassett was right to put constitutional questions at the forefront. By the mid-1920s, a constitutional challenge was brought against the zoning ordinance in Euclid, Ohio. In an attempt to keep out apartments and industry, the small Cleveland suburb had adopted zoning in 1922, restricting the lion's share of the city to single- and two-family homes. The plaintiff was Ambler Realty, the owner of a sixty-eight-acre lot between a major road and rail line primed for industrial use, which had nonetheless been mapped such that large portions of the site could only be used for low-density residential uses. This significantly reduced the value of the site, which the plaintiff alleged constituted an unconstitutional taking. Yet beyond merely challenging the zoning *as applied* in this case, Ambler took the argument a step further, challenging the very constitutionality of zoning.

Beginning in the lower courts, deliberation quickly focused on the most restrictive element of the Euclid zoning code: single-family zoning. In the district court decision, Judge David C. Westenhaver decided on behalf of Ambler Realty, not only finding that the zoning as applied constituted a taking, but blasting zoning's unsubtle intentions:

> The plain truth is that the true object of the ordinance in question is to place all the property in an undeveloped

16 square miles [comprising Euclid, Ohio] in a strait-jacket. . . . The purpose to be accomplished is really to regulate the mode of living of persons who hereinafter inhabit it. In the last analysis, the result to be accomplished is to classify the population and segregate them according to their income or situation in life.[33]

A divided Supreme Court subsequently reversed this decision, dismissing Ambler Realty's takings claims as speculative and upholding the constitutionality of zoning. Apparently moved by a last-minute brief pleading that zoning was merely a kind of nuisance control, the court held zoning to be a legitimate application of police power. The court further held that the exclusionary elements of Euclid's zoning code, such as its sweeping prohibitions on apartments, were not a bug but a feature. In a six–three majority decision, Justice George Sutherland characterized apartments in low-density neighborhoods as "mere parasites." Thus, the constitutionality of zoning—even in its ugliest form—was secured.

The decision in *Euclid* proved to be decisive.[34] With the Supreme Court's stamp of approval and the federal government vigorously promoting its adoption, zoning rapidly spread. By 1930, thirty-five of the then forty-eight states had adopted some form of zoning-enabling legislation, often heavily modeled after SZEA. The Department of Commerce, under the presidencies of both Hoover and Roosevelt, would continue to promote zoning. Between 1926—the year of *Euclid* and the final draft of SZEA—and 1936, zoning would spread rapidly. Indeed, in 1936, the United States Department of Agriculture released and heavily promoted its guidelines for rural zoning, extending zoning beyond its typical urban and suburban domains.

Still, large sections of the country would remain unzoned through World War II. A combination of federal grants and mandates would gradually work to address the remaining holdouts over the next half century. With the Federal Housing Administration underwriting and often outright financing the building boom that followed the war, federal regulators would condition their support—essential to the growth of new suburbs—on the existence of strict zoning controls, such that adopting zoning was often the first act of a newly incorporated suburb.[35] Successive waves of postwar federal housing legislation would provide grants to develop these ordinances. Similar conditions were placed on other federal grants, which surged during the New Deal and again under the Great Society, such that by the end of the 1970s, nearly every city, town, and hamlet in the United States had adopted zoning.

Zoning is not a good institution gone bad. Its purpose is not to address traditional externalities or coordinate growth with infrastructure, as suggested by zoning defenders and envisioned in the sanitized *SimCity* version of city planning. On the contrary, zoning is a mechanism of exclusion designed to inflate property values, slow the pace of new development, segregate cities by race and class, and enshrine the detached single-family house as the exclusive urban ideal—always has been. So, what exactly *is* this system that we have inherited? How does it work today? And what does all this mean for American cities? We turn to these questions in the next chapter.

CHAPTER 2

How Zoning Works

When I started my first planning job in New York City, like all new planners, I was expected to man the zoning help desk at least one day each month. It's an important rite of passage for entry-level planners. In many cities, this is the front line of planning, where anyone and everyone can call in with a zoning question and get help from a planner. Some of my colleagues loathed the work, and not without reason: it takes your full attention, and a good deal of the inquiries come from people who are either mad at you (homeowners) or trying to off-load their work on to you (real estate brokers).

I nonetheless came to love it, volunteering for desk duty many months after it was required. In a job where projects can stretch on for years, there was something invigorating about solving an issue in a matter of minutes. After a week writing dry reports and managing emails, nothing rekindles the spirit of public service like helping someone work through a problem. On top of all of that, having to field dozens of questions each day helps you to come to understand the messy reality of zoning, which is why desk duty was expected of new hires.

The main thing I learned at the help desk is that most people don't know the first thing about zoning. Take a call I received from a lady who lived along Staten Island's eastern shore. In a harried voicemail, she explained her circumstances: She was trying to sell her home. She told the broker to list it as in the neighborhood of Dongan Hills, but the broker said that wasn't allowed. According to the broker, our agency had "rezoned" her home from Dongan Hills to South Beach, so that's what must go in the listings. The questions came frantically at the end: When did your agency "rezone" me into another neighborhood? Why did you do that? And can you "rezone" me back?

At first, I was bewildered. I had never heard of zoning designating specific neighborhoods—this certainly wasn't the case in New York City. Could she be referring to some other change in local zoning? The zoning in that area of Staten Island hadn't changed in over fifty years. Maybe she had in mind some special purpose district? That wasn't it either. At a loss, I decided to give her a call. After hearing the spiel for a second time, with added flavor about how she had lived in the neighborhood her entire life, I gently explained that zoning doesn't designate neighborhoods.

"Well then, which agency assigned me my neighborhood?" she asked.

"I'm not sure that anyone did," I said. "These things just emerge."

Needless to say, that answer wasn't satisfactory.

"Well then, how do I know what neighborhood I live in?" she asked in exasperation.

By this point, the call no longer had anything to do with zoning. But she seemed genuinely worried, so I decided to work with her. Knowing almost nothing about the area, I pulled up Google Maps and plugged in her address.

"According to the label on Google Maps, you live in Dongan Hills," I said.

"Where does that label come from?" she asked.

"I'm not sure. Let me put this to you a different way. Do you live near the Dongan Playground?" I asked

"Yep, I went to elementary school right next door," she said.

"And you live quite close to Dongan Hills Avenue, right?" I asked.

"It's on the other side of Buel Avenue, but yeah, it's about ten minutes away," she said.

"Well, based on the weight of evidence, it sounds to me like you live in Dongan Hills," I explained.

After a sigh of relief on her end, we chatted a little more and (at her request) I coached her on how to explain all of this to her domineering broker. First call of the day done.

On a typical day, a zoning help desk attendant fields at least a half dozen calls like this that have absolutely nothing to do with zoning. Trash is piling up on the vacant lot down the street, what gives? Sorry, that's not zoning; call the folks over in sanitation. The bakery on the ground floor of my building is making too much noise, can you shut them up? Oh, that's not zoning; you will have to make a noise complaint over 311. My neighbor painted his house pink, how is that even legal? Talk to your homeowners' association, because zoning doesn't handle that. If there's one lesson that stuck with me, it's that most people—even some professionals in the field, such as brokers, attorneys, and developers—have only the faintest idea of what zoning does.

My sense is that most people think that zoning and city planning are synonymous. Among the more informed lot, there might even be some vague sense that zoning is a catchall for how cities regulate land. The reality is that zoning does both far less and far more than it does in the popular imagination. To understand the problems with zoning, you will first need to know what it is and what it isn't. In this chapter, we deal with the former; for a wonky exploration of the broader planning ecosystem beyond zoning—which regulates everything from stormwater runoff to building safety—interested readers are encouraged to check out the appendix.

At a basic level, zoning is how government regulates land uses and densities on private land in most US cities and suburbs. That is to say, zoning controls how big of a building you can build on a particular lot, and whether you can use that building for any given residential, commercial, or industrial use. Zoning is administered by local governments, based on the standards handed down to them by state governments. The key document is the zoning map, which assigns all of the land in a city to one of many zoning districts. An associated zoning text informs this map, detailing everything that you can and cannot do in every given zoning district.[1]

The most important thing that these zoning districts do is set out the permitted types of land uses, and the densities at which you are allowed to build without much added review. Your local zoning code will also typically set out how much parking is required for any given combination of use and density. Certain mechanisms, such as variances and special permits, allow property owners to request relief from certain rules in special circumstances. Other mechanisms allow the zoning map or the zoning text to be changed over time. The past thirty years have seen a flurry of reforms designed to add flexibility, at the cost of further complicating the system.

Simple enough, right? Maybe we should unpack all of that.

How Zoning Is Born

While zoning is often thought of as a local institution, it starts with your state's legislature. Subject to certain standards, state enabling legislation authorizes local governments, including municipalities and counties, to undertake the work of segregating uses and controlling densities. These bills come with strict rules controlling how local governments adopt and administer zoning. As we discussed in the last chapter, they are often modeled after legislation drafted by the federal government in the 1920s—yes, even in the 2020s.

Once delegated the powers, local policymakers may adopt zoning. The process will vary by state, but usually a local council will delegate the drafting and maintenance of zoning to a planning commission. In cities and large suburbs, this commission will in turn oversee a planning agency, which maintains a staff of full-time planners. In small towns or suburbs, much of this work will be farmed out to planning consultants. These professional planners will develop the zoning, to be approved by the planning commission and given legal force by the local council. Within the guardrails set by state enabling legislation, local planners have wide latitude in how they write the code, meaning that zoning can vary from municipality to municipality.[2]

While newly incorporated suburbs in growing states like Texas and Arizona are still undergoing this process, most local governments adopted zoning many decades ago. If you live in a city or large suburb, chances are that your local zoning was written between 1920 and 1970. In New York City, for example, the current zoning code was written in 1961. This isn't to say that local zoning never changes; in theory, cities should regularly overhaul their zoning, and in practice, rapidly growing cities and suburbs often do. But the heart and soul of most local codes remains locked in the mid-twentieth century, when the vast majority of zoning codes were adopted.

Decoding the City

What exactly is that planning commission adopting? Zoning can be broken out into two key documents. The first is the zoning map, which assigns every parcel in the city to a zoning district. The color of these districts denotes the uses allowed in each district. Generally speaking, yellow stands for residential, red stands for commercial, and purple stands for industrial. You may also occasionally see green, which usually denotes a park or open space, and blue, which usually denotes public institutions like universities and hospitals. Each of these districts will also have a label, often a letter and a number, which tells you the allowed uses and densities.

Historically, these zoning maps were large paper documents stored in planning offices, but increasingly, they can be found online as interactive maps. Most cities now even have a feature allowing you to plug in your address and find the relevant districts controlling where you live. If you have never looked at your city's zoning map, take a moment to go play around with it. What zoning district do you live in? What are the more common zoning districts in your city? How are they distributed?

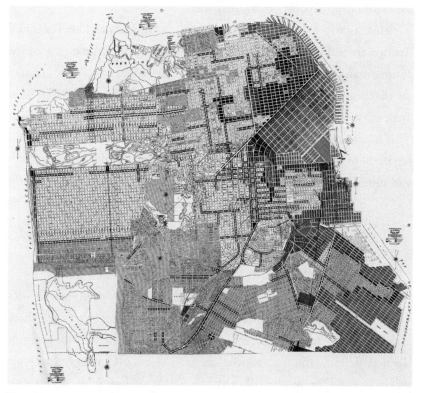

The 1921 zoning map for San Francisco. While simpler than a contemporary zoning map, the broad themes are there, with commercial (black) and industrial (crosshatch) mapped downtown and along corridors, and low-rise residential zones (white and diagonal lines) mapped to cover the remainder of the city. (Erica_Fischer on Flickr)

The second key document is the zoning text. This is the actual ordinance that sets out what you can and cannot do in any given zoning district. It also establishes the process for mechanisms to grant property owners more flexibility or change the zoning map and text—more on these later. The structure of zoning ordinances can vary, so it is hard to generalize. But in most cases, the most important section is the "Definitions" section, which comes early in the text. It's here that you will find the key terms that you will need to understand your local zoning regime.

While I encourage you to play around with your city's zoning map, approach your city's zoning text with caution. Depending on your city, this can be a document stretching hundreds if not thousands of pages long, written in dry legalese, with few charts or illustrations to guide you along your way. Neither I nor Island Press can be held liable for any emotional distress you experience while trying to make heads or tails of your local zoning code!

Everything in Its Right Place

So what exactly is all this meant to regulate? While definitions may vary in superficial ways, zoning regulates two elements: use and density. Use refers to the types of things that you are allowed to do on a property. Zoning broadly reduces cities to three principal uses: residential, commercial, and industrial. This basic breakdown is often denoted by the letter in the district's name, with *R* indicating that it's a residential zone, *C* indicating that it's a commercial zone, and so on. Most cities define special zones for large and unusual land uses, such as university campuses, hospital complexes, and amusement parks.

From here, most cities further break out the main three use categories into a dizzying array of specific subcategories. Residential, for example, will often be broken out into districts for detached single-family houses, attached single-family houses, duplexes, triplexes, fourplexes, and larger apartment buildings. Commercial zoning works in a similar way, with districts distinguishing between uses like small neighborhood retail, regional shopping centers, and professional offices. Industrial zoning is typically less involved, with districts only distinguishing between light and heavy industry.

Each zoning district will explicitly list out all of the allowed uses. In the case of residential districts, this can be quite simple: apartments may be allowed in this district but not that district. Commercial and industrial districts tend to be much more involved, with planners attempting to list out and assign every conceivable use; this is occasionally funny, frequently absurd, and always confusing.

In my hometown of Lexington, Kentucky, the B-1 Neighborhood Business Zone alone lists out forty-seven principal uses, ten accessory uses, and nineteen conditional uses.[3] That means forty-seven kinds of commercial uses—ranging from restaurants to rehabilitation centers—are allowed to operate on their own without any additional review, ten are allowed to operate in conjunction with one of those principal uses, and nineteen may only operate after receiving a special permit.[4] As a result, new business formulas, or businesses that blur these lines in any way, often face substantial permitting hurdles.

Historically, most zoning use regulations were hierarchical, meaning that less intense uses—such as houses—could be in zones designed for more intense uses—such as industry—but not the other way around, with detached single-family housing sitting at the top of the hierarchy. This allowed for some use mixing while still heavily restricting development in low-density residential zones. Today, most American cities enforce flat zoning, meaning that only the explicitly permitted uses are allowed in each zoning district.[5] That is to say, you can only have housing in residential districts and industry in industrial districts.

This strict use segregation is a defining feature of American zoning. Generally speaking, the typical city is zoned to restrict offices and storefronts downtown, a mix of commercial and industrial along key corridors, and low-density residential everywhere else. These low-density residential districts are invariably the strictest: even innocuous uses traditionally found in older suburbs, like corner delis and doctors' offices, are now usually prohibited. Affordable housing typologies—like apartments or manufactured housing—are usually used to buffer affluent neighborhoods from industrial and commercial uses, when they are allowed at all. And while a small but growing number of cities are experimenting with mixed-use zoning, these districts rarely cover much more than 5 percent of a municipality's developable area. The lion's share of a typical zoning map will be covered by low-density residential districts, allowing nothing other than detached, single-family houses.[6]

Don't Be Dense

In addition to each district being given a use designation, it will also have its own density designation. In the district name, this is normally denoted as the number that follows the letter.[7] These rules collectively serve to control the size and shape of the building. In other explanations of zoning, you may see this broken out into other categories, such as height, bulk, and area, but for our purposes, they can safely be understood as variations on the theme of density.

The key density regulation in more urban areas is floor area ratio, or FAR, which restricts how much floor area can be built, presented as a multiple of the lot size. For example, if you own a ten thousand square foot lot that is assigned an FAR of 2, you cannot build more than twenty thousand square feet of floor area.[8] A host of other regulations will then control how you can build out all that floor area:

- Maximum height restricts how tall a building can be.
- Various setback rules, which are also called yards, control how close a building can sit to the front, side, and rear property lines.
- Maximum lot coverage limits the percentage of the lot that can be occupied by a building.

Collectively, these rules determine what is called the envelope, or the three-dimensional space that a building is allowed to take up. Now that you know all this, go take a walk around your neighborhood. Are all the buildings in your neighborhood the exact same height? Are all the front yards the same depth? If you live in a neighborhood built after the 1920s, you may be looking at the regimenting effect of zoning.

Beyond defining the envelope, three other common zoning rules serve to restrict density. First, zoning controls the dimensions of residential lots, including lot size and lot width. Minimum lot size rules require that you set aside so much land per unit of housing. The standard minimum lot size for a detached single-family house in the United States is around five thousand square feet.[9] In more restrictive municipalities, this minimum can go much higher. In much of New England, for example, minimum lot sizes are typically measured in acres rather than in square feet. Minimum lot width rules work in a similar way,

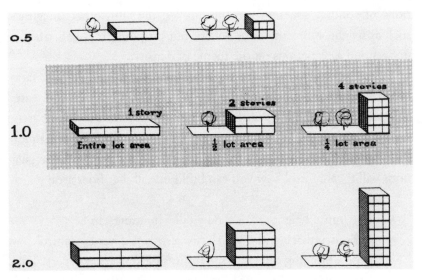

An illustration of how floor area ratio (FAR) rules work; the permitted FAR is in the column on the left. (Courtesy Boston City Archives)

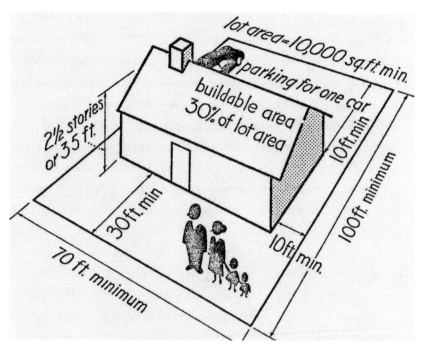

An illustration of the density restrictions in effect in a typical R-1 single-family housing district. Note the idealized family in the front lawn, a reflection of the social vision underwriting zoning. (City of Portland, Oregon Archives, Council Ordinance 110103, 2001-07, 1959)

defining the minimum amount of street frontage that a lot must have. Occasionally, these rules will be hidden away in a separate subdivision ordinance—which you can learn about in the appendix—but they usually reside in the zoning code.

Second, zoning controls the permitted number of units per square feet of floor area. As with minimum lot sizes, these rules usually only apply to residential development and are designed to restrict residential densities. These rules can take many forms. In New York City, where this is called the dwelling unit factor, one common zoning district allows no more than one housing unit per 870 square feet of floor area in the building. This means that if you have an 8,700-square-foot building, it cannot host more than ten units. Importantly, this is different from—and often far more restrictive than—the minimum unit size set out in the building code. While the building code standard will be based on health and safety considerations, the zoning cap is largely arbitrary.[10]

Finally, zoning defines minimum parking requirements for all uses. In residential districts, this usually takes the form of requiring a certain number of parking spaces per unit of housing. In commercial and industrial districts, things get much more complicated, with parking requirements usually defined as one space per a given square feet of floor area, modified for every conceivable commercial and industrial use. These standards are often detailed well past the point of absurdity. In Phoenix, religious communities must provide one parking space per fifty-eight linear inches of pew space.[11] In Charlotte, bar owners must provide one parking space per seventy-five square feet of floor area.[12] So much for combating drunk driving!

How Zoning Changes

Collectively, these use and density rules restrict what can be built where—and to what extent—everywhere in the zoned city. As you can probably imagine, these rules are often poorly suited to reality. According to one study, a startling 40 percent of buildings in Manhattan couldn't be built today, owing mainly to density restrictions.[13] The same is true of most cities that were built out before zoning, including colonial cities such as Savannah or Annapolis. Mercifully, few cities today expect these buildings to be demolished. If the use or density is harmless—such as a slightly tall apartment building—it will be treated as legally nonconforming, meaning it can continue to operate, but not expand. If the nonconforming use or density imposes a burden on neighbors—such as certain disruptive businesses like bars—the owner may be forced to close down operations after a specified amortization period.

In most cities, if a project complies with all of the use and density rules, it can be built as-of-right, meaning that no additional review is necessary beyond the standard building permitting process. But many cities will also allow developers to apply to build projects that don't follow the letter of the zoning code, subject to certain standards. This is called discretionary permitting, as these permits may be issued at the discretion of a local legislative body or zoning board, occasionally after an environmental review and multiple public hearings. This type of discretionary permitting is increasingly the norm within US land-use planning; indeed, in cities like San Francisco and in many suburbs, virtually all permitting is now discretionary.

There are a few traditional ways of getting relief from zoning. First, a variance can grant added flexibility when certain requirements—typically having to do with the building envelope or site dimensions—create an undue hardship for the owner for a specific site. A classic example of this is a site with an extreme grade change: if, let's say, your one-hundred-foot-deep lot is bisected by a large cliff, abiding by the typical thirty-foot front setback might make development of the lot impossible. In this case, a zoning board of appeals may grant you a variance to bypass the front setback rules.[14] In theory, variances were supposed to be used only for outlier cases. In practice, given how restrictive zoning has become, many major cities process hundreds of variance applications per year.[15]

The second mechanism, a special permit, allows a specific development to depart from the standard zoning, subject to strict conditions. Unlike variances, which almost exclusively apply to envelope issues, special permits can modify both the use and density rules to which a site is subject. A common example of a use allowed only via special permit is a parking garage: since a poorly planned parking garage is bound to create a lot of traffic, the zoning code may only allow them pursuant to a site plan showing how the applicant intends to minimize congestion. A typical density special permit might allow a building to rise slightly taller in exchange for a plaza on the ground floor. As you might have guessed, special permits are sometimes about actual harm mitigation and sometimes about extracting unrelated benefits out of an applicant.[16]

Despite originally being sold as a way to bring certainty to the process of regulating urban land, your local zoning is constantly changing in minor ways. This happens via one of two mechanisms. First, through a rezoning, which is an amendment to the zoning map. More often than not, this involves a developer asking the city to reassign their lot to another zoning district so they may build a larger building or accommodate a currently prohibited use. This is called an upzoning, as it increases the development potential of a site. The opposite, in which the development potential for a site is decreased, is called a downzoning. Downzonings are usually deployed as a way to block development.

As with so much of zoning, there is a wide gap between the theory and practice of zoning. In theory, the zoning map is supposed to reflect a rational land-use plan, with some risk that the courts will intervene if cities draw district boundaries without rhyme or reason. Yet in practice, most major cities entertain dozens of rezoning requests a year, redrawing boundaries constantly to accommodate specific projects, resulting in zoning maps that look like a chaotic patchwork of cubes and colors.

For deeper changes to zoning, an applicant may look to a text amendment. This changes the zoning text that informs the districts you see on the zoning map. Depending on what is being changed in the ordinance, a text amendment can adjust what is and is not allowed for all lots in a given district, the process of applying for permits, or the way that zoning should be interpreted. A typical text amendment might modify use or density rules in an established district to respond to changing development trends, or create an entirely new zoning district to accommodate a new type of development.

Two zoning maps covering the exact same territory of New York City in 1961 and 2021, illustrating the exponential increase in complexity of zoning maps. (NYC Department of City Planning)

As with rezonings, text amendments are often a response to specific development applications, which come by the dozens each year in most major cities. But sometimes they reflect broader shifts. For example, during the COVID-19 pandemic, many cities scrambled to amend their zoning codes to accommodate home-based businesses.[17] Whatever the source, extend this type of amendment activity across the half century that most zoning ordinances have been in effect, and the typical zoning text has devolved from clear and concise twenty-page documents into hundreds of pages of hedges, qualifications, and exceptions that can only be interpreted by a trained planner or land-use attorney.[18] Better governed cities respond to this problem by regularly overhauling both the zoning text and map.

Patching Up Zoning?

A number of new mechanisms have sprung up to try and address mounting issues with zoning. Special districts, for example, add an additional layer of rules, or an overlay, on top of the base zoning, modifying either use or density rules. In suburbs, planned unit developments, or PUDs, have emerged as a popular way to give developers of large projects latitude to write their own use and density rules in exchange for substantial exactions, such as infrastructure improvements or conservation easements. In cities, incentive zoning works similarly as a kind of transaction, in that a municipality will allow additional density in exchange for exactions like income-restricted housing or additional contributions to city coffers.

Other reform proposals have been more ambitious. In recent years, form-based codes have been marketed as a way to moderate use regulation and refocus density regulations on mandating an aesthetic that reflects the surrounding built context. But where they have been deployed, as in Miami and Denver, form-based codes have usually meant combining only slightly less strict use rules with much stricter envelope rules.[19] Less successfully, advocates of performance zoning have proposed to shift the focus from lists of uses to measurable impacts. The idea has seen little uptake, beyond the occasional city mandating landscape buffers or adding an additional layer of regulations in industrial districts.[20]

Where successful, these reforms have offered a welcome safety valve, allowing cities and suburbs to bypass a midcentury zoning system poorly suited to twenty-first-century needs and preferences. Yet the underlying problems remain unaddressed: Uses are still segregated and densities are still heavily restricted. Large swathes of most cities remain restricted to detached single-family houses. Commercial and industrial developments continue to be forced into auto-centric form. And for all the rezonings, text amendments, and overlays that get adopted each year, the standard American zoning code remains, at its heart, a code written for another time. As I will argue in part III, moving beyond this paradigm will require more than just a safety valve—it will require a sea change in how we plan land use.

If you are feeling a little overwhelmed, keep in mind two key points. First, zoning regulates uses and densities on private land—nothing more, nothing less. It works principally by what it prevents rather than by what it causes. To the extent that zoning forces anything to be built, it does so only by limiting the options of property owners. Second, zoning varies a lot city by city and is prone to constant change. The best way to understand your local zoning code is to check out your local zoning map, familiarize yourself with the basic zoning districts set out in your local zoning text, and follow local zoning applications in the news as they happen. As you explore the world of city planning—and as I discuss in greater detail in the appendix—you will soon find that a surprising amount of it has little to do with zoning.

Part II

CHAPTER 3

Planning an Affordability Crisis

Until recently, zoning was a sleepy backwater in the policy world. Outside of a handful of local government policy wonks, land-use attorneys, and planning consultants, the rules controlling where and how Americans lived attracted little attention. Local policymakers in turn relished and feared the powers that this strange system bequeathed upon them. Where media coverage of zoning existed at all, it was mostly limited to the occasional write-up of a local fight by an uninterested journalist assigned to the local government beat. If a layperson knew anything about zoning at all, chances are they didn't have an opinion about it.

That slowly started to change over the course of the 2010s. As interest in land-use regulation rekindled among urban economists in the early 2000s, researchers began to find increasingly clear evidence of a link between high housing costs and zoning.[1] A trickle of blogs and e-books would bring popular attention to the issue.[2] In 2014, ideas turned into activism, with the nation's first YIMBY (Yes In My Backyard) groups emerging seemingly out of nowhere in the Bay Area, on a mission to fight for housing and rein in zoning.

In short order, the movement spread nationwide, with dozens of groups fighting for zoning liberalization at the state and local levels across the country as of 2022. By decade's end, both the Obama and Trump administrations had vowed to take on zoning reform.[3] Editorials decrying the evils of zoning now find their way into the opinion sections of national newspapers on a weekly basis. Once ignored, the relationship between zoning and high housing costs has become enshrined as common sense.[4] Indeed, I suspect it's why you picked up this book.

And it's true: our most productive cities spent the past fifty years using zoning to prevent new housing supply from meeting demand, resulting in an affordability crisis. While housing affordability has long been an issue for those at the bottom of the housing market, it has recently evolved into an issue affecting nearly every American. Shocking data points to this effect abound. Between 1970 and 2010, median home values appreciated at a rate of nearly three times median household incomes, particularly in prospering coastal cities.[5] Today, half of all American renters are rent-burdened—spending over a third of their income on rent—and one in four American renters is severely rent-burdened—spending over half of their income on rent.[6] These figures have only worsened over the course of the COVID-19 pandemic, with supply shortages driving up housing prices at the highest rate since the crisis years of the late 1970s.[7]

But what *exactly* is the mechanism by which zoning increases housing costs? There are three. The most obvious way is by blocking new housing altogether, whether by prohibiting affordable housing or through explicit rules restraining densities. This results in less housing being built, resulting in the supply-demand mismatches we see in most US cities today. A subtler way that zoning drives up housing costs is by forcing the housing that *is* built to be of a higher quality than residents might otherwise require, through policies such as minimum lot sizes or minimum parking requirements. Beyond these written prohibitions and mandates, zoning often raises housing costs simply by adding an onerous and unpredictable layer of review to the permitting process.

While zoning has always been restrictive, the rules that we place on land uses and densities have become exponentially stricter since roughly 1960. In built-out cities along the coasts, zoning makes redevelopment much more difficult, such that many municipalities have effectively stopped building altogether. New York City, for example, built fewer new units in the recovery boom of the 2010s than it did in the Great Depression of the 1930s.[8] In the smaller suburbs that dot regions like the great bays of California and Massachusetts, zoning has emerged as an effective tool for blocking any and all development, locking many communities in amber.

As a result, many coastal housing markets now operate in a context of permanent housing crisis. Relatively little housing is built, and where it is built at all, the housing is kept prohibitively expensive by unnecessary mandates and a costly permitting process.[9] With restrictive zoning already on the books in those cities that remain somewhat affordable—usually thanks to an increasingly scarce supply of undeveloped land—the housing affordability crisis is unlikely to remain an exclusively coastal phenomenon for long. What happens when cities like Austin and Denver—both already posting some of the highest housing price appreciation in the country—run out of developable land within an hour's drive of downtown? Absent zoning reform, the housing affordability crisis is only going to get much, much worse in the years to come.

Zoned Out

The first way that zoning makes housing more expensive is by allowing less of it to be built. This gets to the heart of the housing affordability problem, which is fundamentally a mismatch between supply and demand: a lot of people need homes, but not enough new homes are being built, resulting in high and rising prices for existing homes. These needed new homes aren't going unbuilt because of developer ignorance or a lack of land—developers are champing at the bit to build in expensive cities, and we have the technology to build up when we can't build out. They're going unbuilt because of zoning.

In nearly every major US city, apartments are banned outright in at least 70 percent of residential areas. In suburbs, this share is often much higher, if apartments aren't banned altogether. In San Jose, incidentally one of America's most unaffordable cities, apartments are banned in 94 percent of residential areas. That is to say, the most you can build in virtually every US residential neighborhood is a detached single-family home.[10] No building new apartments, no subdividing existing homes.[11] Where cities might historically have followed a growth trajectory taking them from farms to homes to duplexes to small apartment buildings to large apartment buildings, zoning locks the overwhelming majority of residential neighborhoods into that second stage.[12]

When zoning *does* allow apartments to be built, many codes place explicit caps on the number of residential units that a given lot can host. In New York City, for example, zoning regulations restrict the number of apartments that can be subdivided within a building, not out of any health and safety concerns, but simply to restrict housing production. In many cities, such as Los Angeles, this artificial cap on housing takes the form of the number of units permitted per acre of land, but the effect is the same: zoning places an arbitrary limit on the number of homes a particular piece of land may host, regardless of housing demand or building capabilities.

Beyond explicit apartment bans, a host of regulations controlling massing—or the physical space that a building can take up—likewise limit how much housing can be built on any particular lot. Most people may know about height limits. But behind the scenes, rules like minimum setbacks and maximum floor area ratios (FARs) severely limit the

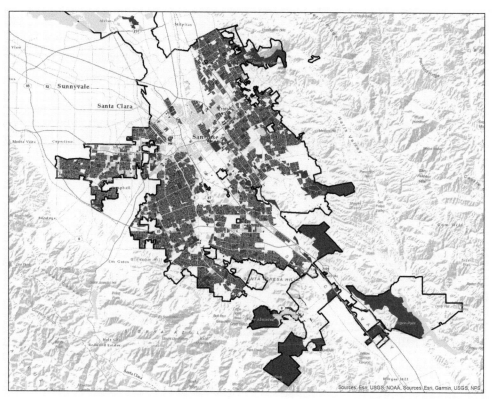

A residential zoning map of San Jose. The lighter shade denotes pockets where multifamily residential is allowed; the darker shade denotes areas deemed appropriate for residential uses but strictly limited to detached single-family housing. (M. Nolan Gray)

development potential of most residential areas.[13] For example, in Frankfort, Kentucky, the sparingly mapped "High Density Multifamily" zone limits buildings to 30 percent lot coverage and requires the provision of 750 square feet of open space per apartment, while imposing an onerous minimum lot size of 6,000 square feet, plus 1,600 square feet for each additional apartment.[14] If an apartment built to those specifications pencils at all in a typical inner suburb of Frankfort, it will host very few units.

In addition to heavily restricting apartments, many zoning codes ban the most affordable housing typologies outright. In cities, this means prohibiting single-room occupancies, or SROs, in which residents rent a furnished private bedroom with shared kitchen and bathroom facilities. Where they are allowed, SROs serve as the bottom rung of the housing market, providing exceptionally affordable accommodations to low-income singles, including seniors and recent arrivals to the city.[15]

In the postwar period, however, many cities modified their zoning to either ban SROs or make them technically infeasible. In 1955, New York City took the former route and spent the next two decades heavily subsidizing their conversion into hotels and luxury condominiums. Similar policies played out across the country. With few other urban housing options serving the most vulnerable, this seemingly modest zoning change has played no small role in driving the contemporary homelessness crisis facing cities.[16]

If SROs serve as the bottom rung of the housing market in cities, manufactured homes—or, if you prefer, trailers or mobile homes—fill a similar niche in suburban and rural markets. Particularly in warmer and more temperate environs across the Sun Belt and along the West Coast, manufactured housing offers affordable and stable shelter for working-class families.[17] This is particularly true of seasonal workers in agriculture and the energy sector, where mobility comes with a premium.

Yet, as with SROs, many suburban and rural zoning codes outright ban manufactured housing. Indeed, it's not uncommon to find suburban and rural municipalities in states like Florida that incorporated strictly so they could adopt zoning and prohibit manufactured housing. As with apartments, where cities allow manufactured homes at all, they usually zone them to be hidden away within industrial districts, forcing the mixture of incompatible uses that zoning is theoretically tasked with preventing.

The cover story for the adoption of many of these zoning rules, where planners even bothered to come up with one, was to improve the lives of the most vulnerable. Given the choice, who would choose to live in a small apartment, or an SRO, or a trailer park? Who wouldn't want a big yard, or a private kitchen, or a large home? The trouble is that banning affordable housing doesn't make expensive housing any more accessible. By putting a floor on housing markets, zoning has merely locked out everyone who cannot clear that floor. Such a policy puts those with means on a treadmill of ever-higher rents and those without means on the streets. As the benefits to living in a prosperous city continue to grow and more dollars flood in to bid up the prices of the existing supply of housing, this zoning-induced crisis will only get worse.

Mandating Mansions

For every rule explicitly prohibiting or restricting new housing, a half dozen rules force those houses and apartments that are built to be far more expensive than residents might otherwise prefer. This is the second principal way that zoning raises housing costs. To the extent that these mandates allow fewer units to be built (as with minimum lot sizes) or make many units financially or physically infeasible (as with minimum parking requirements), this category could be seen as a subset of the first way that zoning raises housing costs.

One such set of zoning regulations that raises housing costs are minimum lot sizes, which put a floor on how much land developers must set aside for each home built. These rules are most common in single-family zoning districts, where lot size can be a major driver of costs. While minimum lot size rules may have some health and safety justification in rural areas where sewer hookups aren't yet available—you need space for residents to safely use septic—these rules serve no purpose other than to drive up housing costs and drive down population densities in most urban and suburban communities. For this reason, early research into the use of zoning toward exclusionary ends zeroed in on minimum lot sizes for their capacity to substantially raise housing costs.[18]

Consider how this works out in a fairly simple development scenario: Imagine that a developer hopes to build a subdivision on just under three acres, or 120,000 square feet, of land. Let's assume that subdivision regulations require that a quarter of the land must go toward streets and a small community park, leaving 90,000 square feet of land for houses. After an extensive market study, the developer finds that there is a strong market for starter homes on modest 5,000-square-foot lots. That means they could develop and sell a total of eighteen homes.

Now imagine that the suburb this developer is working in imposes a minimum lot size of 7,500 square feet. This would have two implications: for starters, our developer would now only be able to build twelve homes. But in addition to losing six homes, the remaining twelve homes would also be more expensive. Since land accounts for roughly a third of the value of a home, and the city is using zoning to force land consumption to increase by 50 percent, the cost of the remaining twelve homes would need to increase by at least 15 percent. For a $175,000 starter home, that adds nearly $30,000 to the final cost. At best, we are left with twelve more expensive homes. At worst, this market can't yet sustain this higher price point, and no units are built at all.

If minimum lot size regulations are an important driver of high housing costs in suburbs, minimum parking requirements fill this role in cities.[19] Concerning housing, minimum parking requirements mandate that for each unit of housing built, a developer must also build a specified number of off-street parking spaces. While a developer has the incentives and local knowledge to make an educated guess at how much parking a particular project actually requires—if they supply too few spaces, they can't lease or sell the units; if they build too many spaces, they lose money—minimum parking requirements supersede this judgment with arbitrary standards.

The word *arbitrary* is not used lightly. These rules bear little relation to reality and often work in strange ways. In my hometown of Lexington, Kentucky, to use an all too typical example, a single-family home must provide 1 off-street parking space. But a duplex must provide 4 off-street parking spaces. An apartment building must provide 1.5 off-street parking spaces per unit or 0.9 spaces per bedroom, whichever is greater.[20] Curiously, the zoning mandates *more* off-street parking for those housing typologies most likely to be affordable and urban—that is to say, those hosting residents *least* likely to own a car. Call that what you will, but that's not planning.

The housing affordability implications of minimum parking requirements can be serious, particularly in the case of multifamily housing. In the best of cases, where land is abundant and cheap, minimum parking requirements usually result in an unsightly surface parking lot. As with minimum lot sizes, this effectively mandates that each resident consumes more land, raising the cost of housing. If Lexington's minimum parking requirements were to apply to a 675-square-foot, two-bedroom apartment, for example, it would double the amount of space that each resident is forced to consume.[21] Even where land costs are low, this mandate will not come cheap.

These mandates can quickly escalate in cost where land constraints require the construction of a parking structure. In cities like Miami and New Orleans, where flooding is a major risk, this may entail a parking podium that towers over the street. In cities like Washington, DC, and Los Angeles, this may involve extensive—and expensive—excavation. In either case, the added costs of a mandated parking garage to residents can be substantial: one estimate puts the added cost to each unit at around $50,000.[22] For a condo that might otherwise have cost

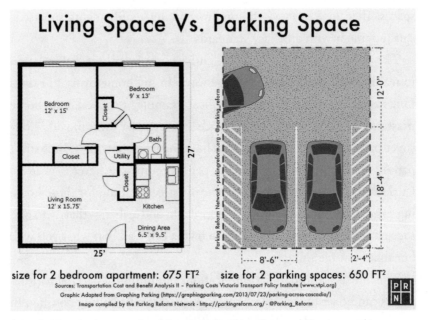

Living Space Vs. Parking Space

Bedroom
12' x 15'

Bedroom
9' x 13'

Closet

Closet

Bath

Closet

Utility

Living Room
12' x 15.75'

Closet

Kitchen

Dining Area
6.5' x 9.5'

25'

27'

12'-0"

18'-4"

8'-6"

2'-4"

Parking Reform Network - parkingreform.org - @parking_reform

size for 2 bedroom apartment: 675 FT²   size for 2 parking spaces: 650 FT²

Sources: Transportation Cost and Benefit Analysis II – Parking Costs Victoria Transport Policy Institute (www.vtpi.org)
Graphic Adapted from Graphing Parking (https://graphingparking.com/2013/07/23/parking-across-cascadia/)
Image compiled by the Parking Reform Network - https://parkingreform.org/ - @Parking_Reform

PR
N

A modest two-bedroom unit and its required parking. By mandating two parking spaces, as many zoning codes do, minimum parking requirements dramatically increase the cost of housing. (Parking Reform Network)

$150,000, this can increase the final price by a third. As with minimum lot sizes, at best you get a more expensive home. At worst, the project doesn't pencil and you get no housing at all.

Housing Delayed Is Housing Denied

Beyond these written prohibitions and mandates, zoning also raises costs by subjecting many new developments to an opaque permitting process that can substantially increase the cost of a new apartment or home. Under many circumstances, development happens as-of-right. That is to say, if the proposal is fully compliant with the current zoning, the city must issue permits after a standard review by the building department—no haggling with regulators, no public review. This creates a high degree of certainty about what can and can't be built and minimizes the headache associated with building new housing.[23]

The trouble is that zoning today throws many developments out of this as-of-right process and into a prolonged, expensive, and unpredictable shadow permitting process. This can happen in one of two ways. First, by conditioning development on special permits. While this added layer of review may be reasonable with certain exceptional projects, cities increasingly condition even run-of-the-mill developments on the receipt of special permits. Second, by a developer needing to request a variance or a rezoning. Because contemporary zoning is so restrictive, more and more projects must request either a more liberal zoning designation—a rezoning—or an exemption to certain rules—a variance—to make housing feasible at all.

Whatever the cause may be, being thrown into an extended public review can raise the cost of new housing in various subtle ways. For starters, there are the added fees. In most major cities, these added costs are non-negligible. In Los Angeles, for example, a simple variance will run you $13,283, while a special permit that requires approval from the city planning commission will cost a hefty $32,212.[24] This leaves out the cost of hiring a land-use attorney with local connections, whom the applicant will need to walk them through this process, thereby adding tens of thousands of dollars to the process.

Then there is the environmental review, which in certain states is required for various types of zoning permits. These reviews can be startlingly complex, even for simple projects. On one project I worked on as the lead planner in New York City—a rezoning to legalize an *existing* doctor's office—the environmental assessment ran 130 pages. On another project—a rezoning to allow a midrise apartment building near a subway station—it ran close to 500 pages. In both cases, needless to say, no significant environmental impacts were found.[25] Yet if project opponents had been so motivated, they could have dragged either project to court by second-guessing these reports, adding thousands of dollars in legal costs and months of delay to the process.

Onerous though these charges may at first seem, these up-front costs are easy to manage. Where things get hairy are the delays. Depending on the local zoning ordinance, securing a rezoning or a special permit can easily add months, if not years, of public review. In New York City, for example, the fastest you can get through public review for a rezoning or a special permit is roughly seven and a half months. When you add in the necessary year of back-and-forth negotiating with planners and elected officials before public review even starts, the process from start to finish runs closer to two years. Worse yet, this reasonably clear timeline is perhaps the best-case scenario: particularly in the suburbs, public review will usually follow no timeline at all, with the applicant returning for additional hearings on an indefinite basis.

Beyond merely delaying the completion of housing that is needed sooner rather than later, these procedural hurdles add substantial costs to the final project in the form of months and years of added property taxes and maintenance.[26] And all those public hearings have a way of further compounding costs. As Katherine Levine Einstein, David M. Glick, and Maxwell Palmer discuss in their pioneering study of the zoning public review process, negative comments from local residents can nudge the presiding planning or zoning board into forcing the applicant to conduct additional studies of dubious value or limit the scope of the project altogether.[27]

A story the authors tell at the beginning of their book captures how all of this plays out in practice. In late 2016, an applicant in Cambridge, Massachusetts—a town with a debilitating housing shortage—requested permits to convert a warehouse into a small fourplex, with one parking space per unit. After a handful of technical questions on the part of members of the Cambridge Planning Board, a raucous crowd of local residents raised concerns about everything from density to parking to structural integrity. In response, the board mandated that the applicant complete additional parking and geotech engineering studies—which can each run tens of thousands of dollars—and return for a rehearing in three months. At the second hearing, in an attempt to avoid further delays, the applicant offered to scrap one of the units and supply two parking spaces for each remaining unit. By the topsy-turvy standards of American zoning, this outcome was considered a success.

While outcomes like this, in isolation, will hardly remake metropolitan housing markets, the scale of the problem becomes clear when you realize that thousands of zoning fights of this nature play out each year in cities across the country. At a time when many cities and suburbs are in the throes of an unprecedented housing shortage, zoning is systematically stymying as-of-right construction and forcing housing proposals to undergo months of heated public hearings and aimless studies, resulting in fewer housing units at a higher cost, to no discernable public benefit.

Why Did This Happen?

But who are these people who show up to oppose housing? And how did zoning get so restrictive in the first place? As we discussed in the first chapter, zoning was partly sold as a way to inflate the property values of commercial landlords. But up until a half century ago, zoning constituted a relatively minor check on overall housing construction. Even through World War II, many American zoning codes remained somewhat flexible by modern standards, though with due deference paid to the institution's original constituencies. Use categories remained reasonably broad, density restrictions were largely limited to height and lot coverage rules, and nearly all development occurred as-of-right.

This would all begin to unravel as early as the late 1960s, as thousands of cities and suburbs across the country aggressively expanded use segregation, significantly tightened density rules, and imposed months of additional public review on development applications. What changed? The most compelling theory, known as the *homevoter hypothesis*, holds that a mixture of rapid inflation and generous federal tax policies heavily incentivized the treatment of a home as an investment, which in turn provided homeowners with an even stronger incentive to oppose new housing construction.[28]

As set out by urban economist Bill Fischel, the argument unfurls as follows. Beginning in the mid-1960s, inflation crept up and remained high through the 1970s, hitting a year-over-year peak of 13.3 percent in 1979.[29] At the same time, the federal government enforced a tax code that heavily favored homeownership, with generous deductions for mortgage interest payments and the capital gains made off of home value appreciation. As a result, many Americans parked their life savings into their home. Once a consumption good, the home became an investment vehicle, with homeowners now bought into a system of zoning that guaranteed the value of their principal investment. It was thus during the 1970s that land-use regulation became exponentially stricter. While inflation has subsided and recent tax reforms have slightly reduced the federal subsidy to homeowners, the vicious cycle of treating housing as an investment, supporting exclusionary zoning to prop up its value, and watching home values rise has only deepened over the past half century.[30]

If the homevoter hypothesis holds, it suggests a bleak future for zoning. After all, if the most powerful local constituency—homeowners—is fully bought into the use of regulation to artificially inflate home prices, it will be nearly impossible for local policymakers to reform it. Worse yet, it suggests that where reforms to zoning can slip through the cracks, these gains may be on weak political footing. As we will discuss in part III, it will take deeper reforms than merely amending local zoning codes to dig our way out of the contemporary housing affordability crisis.

‖▌‖

Much of the popular discussion surrounding zoning and housing costs has focused on coastal cities that are already expensive. Understandably so: housing shortages in cities like New York City and San Francisco produce no shortage of visceral news stories, from Dickensian overcrowding to soul-crushing "supercommutes." But this focus on the current crisis likely understates the extent to which zoning threatens housing affordability nationwide.

As more Americans are forced out of today's expensive cities, we are slowly seeing this crisis creep into the interior, as previously affordable cities develop their remaining cheap land and hit the limits of what zoning will allow. From Boise to Tampa, a flood of families priced out of states like California and New York is already having this effect. Housing markets in satellite tech hubs like Boulder and Durham increasingly resemble the crisis in the Bay Area. And the exclusionary zoning of prospering college towns in otherwise struggling regions, such as Madison or Ann Arbor, is already indistinguishable from coastal peers like Berkeley or Cambridge.

Reshuffling Americans into what are temporarily less expensive cities at best just buys us time. Many of the zoning policies detailed in this chapter, from sweeping apartment prohibitions to high minimum parking requirements to permitting delays, are already on the books in most Sun Belt and Mountain West cities. The key difference between cities like Los Angeles and San Antonio, or between Boston and Jacksonville, is that the latter still have undeveloped (and often unzoned) farmland left to be developed.[31] At the rate these cities are growing, that won't remain the case for long. Absent fundamental reforms, the housing affordability crisis will only spread. We treat zoning as a policy backwater at our own peril.

CHAPTER 4

The Wealth We Lost

Ancient Athens, Renaissance Florence, contemporary Silicon Valley. What do they all have in common? Besides profoundly shaping the world we live in today, all three clarify the importance of place in making us more creative, innovative, and productive. From the invention of Western philosophy to the aesthetic highs of the Renaissance to the dizzying pace of technological change in Silicon Valley, genius does not seem to be randomly distributed. Rather, it clusters in particular places at particular times.[1]

Why is that? While few of us will achieve the highs of an Albert Einstein (who was nourished by the intellectual ferment under way in cities like Bern and Zurich) or Alexander Graham Bell (who decamped for Boston to start his pioneering laboratory), cities nonetheless have a way of making each of us slightly better at whatever it is we do. As massive labor markets, cities allow each of us to specialize, or even strike out on our own as entrepreneurs. Your typical city can't sustain the legions of actors and editors needed to constitute a functioning film industry, but in the massive and highly specialized labor markets of Los Angeles, Hollywood is possible.

At the same time, cities facilitate what are called knowledge spillovers. By letting more people work near one another, in the words of economics journalist Ryan Avent, cities act as conduits of information.[2] Over time, cities tend to build up unique bodies of knowledge that can be hard to put into words. As the saying goes, "You had to be there." Almost by osmosis—at parties, over coffee, at professional conferences—cities allow new knowledge to quickly spread. By clustering in a place like Manhattan, for example, financial institutions not only have access to a common pool of highly specialized labor but can also quickly learn from and incorporate the ideas of their Wall Street competitors.

But what does all this have to do with zoning? Maybe you are unmoved by the issue of housing affordability. Perhaps you are realizing that you are one of those "homevoters" discussed in the last chapter, or you live in a part of the country where housing is cheap thanks to plentiful land or low demand. Why should you care about zoning? The simple answer is that the effects of zoning on the housing market don't stop with high rents or expensive houses. By blocking the growth of our most productive cities, zoning is stunting growth and innovation *nationwide*.

Zoning—by way of raising housing costs—has forced millions of Americans to forego heavily zoned, unaffordable cities like Boston and San Jose for more affordable cities like Atlanta and Phoenix. Atlanta and Phoenix are fine cities, don't get me wrong. Indeed, they deserve a lot of credit for embracing the growth that their coastal peers turn away. But the broader economic implications of this misallocation are serious: by forcing more Americans to avoid our most productive cities merely to find a decent home, we may be permanently stunting the growth and innovation that made America prosperous in the first place. Even if you are unmoved by the plight of the coastal renter, you're almost certainly poorer as a result of zoning.

How Cities Make Us Rich

At first glance, cities come with a lot of costs. They're often noisy, dirty, and smelly—especially in the case of New York. If you live in a city, you will pay more money for a smaller living space. If you drive, you will sit in more traffic and pay more for parking. If you take transit, you will be dependent on an often overcrowded and unreliable system. As an economist might describe it, cities come with a lot of negative "external-ities," or spillovers that affect the lives of others. Yet despite these issues, Americans have consistently flowed into cities since our nation's found-ing, such that just over 80 percent of us now live in urban areas. And according to United Nations researchers, an easy majority of the globe now lives in cities.[3] Is half of the human race just crazy?

Maybe they are. Or maybe all those costs are offset by all the benefits that cities bring. After all, cities also come with a lot of positive exter-nalities, or at least enough to offset the negative. For starters, cities give residents choice. Concentrating a lot of people means you can support a diverse array of goods and services, resulting in choice in what we eat and drink, how we dress, and how we entertain ourselves. This choice often holds added importance for marginalized communities: from Jews to homosexuals, persecuted groups throughout history have long found shelter and community in the large, diverse populations that only a city can support.

Cities also make us *much* more productive, which translates into greater wealth. Economists refer to these productivity gains as "agglom-eration effects." Some of these effects are obvious: by eliminating dis-tance, cities reduce transportation costs. All else being equal, a firm can save money by locating close to the firms with whom it buys and sells. This is why the steel industry concentrated so heavily in a city like Pitts-burgh, where the key input—coal—was readily available.[4] This cluster-ing, in turn, drives competition among local producers and consumers, resulting in lower prices and improved output. For all the talk about tele-communications technologies killing face-to-face meetings, as long as firms need to move products or meet in person, there will always be an incentive to minimize distance by clustering in cities.

But a subtler way that cities make our society richer is simply by hosting large labor markets.[5] Imagine an energy engineer. In a small town or a typical city, there may be little to no demand for their labor. But in a metropolitan area with a robust energy sector—such as Houston—there may be multiple firms who could make full use of their skills, bidding up their wages and allowing them to further specialize. With so many options, the young engineer—or designer, or doctor, or accountant—can easily find the position where they can create the most value, job-hopping until they find the perfect fit.[6] Scale this up a few million times, and you can see how the large labor markets that cities host can make us collectively more productive.

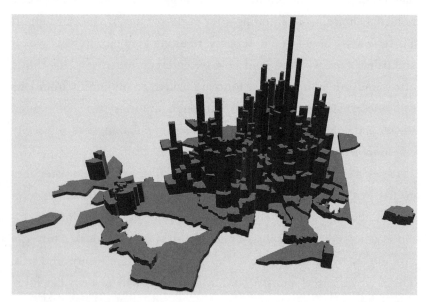

A simplified 3D density gradient of metropolitan San Antonio. Note how even in a city known for its sprawl, densities peak around a central business district and rapidly fall extending outward, with the exception of satellite employment centers. (M. Nolan Gray)

According to urban planner Alain Bertaud, labor markets are so central to explaining why cities exist that they ultimately play a defining role in driving urban form.[7] Why do land prices—and thus densities—universally peak in the traditional core of the city and gradually decline as you move outward?[8] The answer is that firms bid up the cost of land in central locations—such as the Loop in Chicago or Peachtree Center in Atlanta—to tap into the largest labor markets possible. This is particularly true of firms that require highly specialized labor, like research laboratories or corporate headquarters. Residents, in turn, bid up the price of land near these job centers, driving up adjacent densities. These forces explain why cities across the world—despite a dizzying array of local conditions, from Barcelona to Bangkok to Boston—exhibit a pattern of density peaking in a "central business district" and gradually declining outward.

As the urban economist Enrico Moretti notes, all of this also shows up in income data: as city populations grow, incomes—a useful proxy for productivity—also grow. Average wages in cities with at least a million workers are roughly a third higher than in cities with fewer than 250,000 workers.[9] This divergence has only strengthened since 1970 and is likely to continue in the years to come. Why is that? As Moretti and others suggest, it comes down to the fact that our increasingly knowledge-based economy depends on the kind of highly specialized labor that can only be found in large cities.

And then there are knowledge spillovers. As described by Avent, cities act as conduits of information: ideas about how to build better products or run better organizations are "in the air." When a lot of people work near each other, they learn from one another, integrating the innovations of competitors and remixing existing ideas. This is especially true among firms in the same industry, which helps to explain why industries cluster so aggressively, be it automotive engineering in Detroit or music in Nashville. Residents of these cities enjoy access to an accumulated body of knowledge that makes them the best at what they do.[10]

For all the mythology surrounding the lone genius, most innovation emerges from small groups exchanging ideas. Economists have picked up on evidence for such knowledge spillovers in things like academic and patent citations, which reveal that researchers and inventors are far more likely to cite someone physically near them.[11] But the legends surrounding knowledge spillovers perhaps remain more compelling than the data. By one popular account, Silicon Valley—one of America's most innovative economic regions today—owes its birth to computer engineers in the region simply meeting over beers at places like the Wagon Wheel bar in Mountain View, exchanging ideas in groups like the Homebrew Computer Club, and eventually starting new tech titans like Intel.[12]

Approaching cities from a different angle, an interdiciplinary team recently picked up on all of this in the data.[13] Along with collaborators in a range of disciplines, they find that cities become incrementally more innovative as they grow: by one measure, individual productivity rises 15 percent each time a city doubles in size, resulting in a concurrent increase in salaries. The number of inventions and inventors—as evinced by patent data—and the amount of money firms spend on research and development also scale in a superlinear way, meaning that as cities grow, they become even more innovative. Better yet, there is no reason to believe that there is an upper bound to the potential innovation that could come from growing cities.

Beyond specialization and knowledge spillovers, cities also drive innovation to the extent that they foster entrepreneurship. Entrepreneurs require what only a big city can offer: a large potential nearby market, a large labor market to provide the specialized labor they may require, and the ecosystem of business services that young firms depend on. Add in the special sauce of an entrepreneurial culture, and cities transform into engines of growth. All of this innovation gradually transforms into what urban theorist Jane Jacobs calls "new work," remaking the larger economies that surround cities.[14]

All of this innovation makes us collectively wealthier, even if you don't happen to work in an especially innovative sector. Within cities, each new job in a high-tech industry creates five more jobs in various local service sectors, like education, dining, health care, or entertainment.[15] Economists call this a "multiplier" effect, in that the wealth of innovative sectors multiplies into many more jobs, creating opportunity for folks at all levels of the economy. More jobs mean more firms bidding up wages, making everyone from teachers to cooks to doctors to clerks wealthier along the way.[16] This is partly why a bus driver in San Francisco earns twice as much as a bus driver in rural Mississippi.

Even beyond cities, we are all enriched by the innovation and specialization that happens in cities. From the managerial ferment of cities like Seattle and Dallas, we get more efficiently run firms that produce better products and services at cheaper prices. Indeed, many of these advances—from two-day delivery to robust 5G networks—matter even more if you don't live in a city. And the technological innovations that continue to spin out of cities, from cheap smartphones and solar panels to the sequencing of the human genome, speak for themselves. These innovations improve all of our lives, regardless of whether you live in a city or not. For all the noise in recent decades about the death of distance, place matters, and it will continue to matter. Indeed, contrary to all the anti-urban doomsaying at the start of the COVID-19 pandemic, residential rents have largely already recovered by mid-2021, and office rents are poised to follow a similar track.[17]

Zoning for Stagnation

Now more than ever, we should be concerned with cultivating this growth. Consider a few distressing trends. Since the early 1970s, real median wages have essentially flatlined. More broadly, productivity growth has been consistently underwhelming over the past fifty years, other than the occasional wonder out of Silicon Valley. It isn't helping that entrepreneurship fell by roughly 50 percent between 1978 and 2011. Nor is it helping that more Americans are staying put: according to the US Census, moving to a new city or state is at an historic low, with Americans in 2018 moving at less than half the rate they did in 1985.[18]

What exactly is going on? One possibility, set out by Avent, is that high housing costs in a handful of cities—a downstream effect of zoning—are forcing more people and businesses out of our most productive places. The observant reader may note that each of these trends takes a turn for the worse around the time that cities tightened their zoning rules. Was this an accident?

Consider a puzzle: as of 2010, the median household income in San Jose was nearly double that of Orlando. That is to say, a worker in San Jose is potentially twice as productive as a worker in Orlando. Yet between 2010 and 2020, Orlando's population grew at *four times* the rate of San Jose's. On its face, this is a bizarre outcome: under normal conditions, we would expect mobility trends to be reversed, with workers pouring into San Jose, which also happens to be America's wealthiest big city. Why aren't Americans moving to where their labor can command the highest wages?[19]

You most likely already know the answer: housing costs. The median home price in San Jose is *four times* as expensive as in Orlando.[20] The sad reality is that, in San Jose, all of those additional earnings would be erased by astronomical rents or a steep mortgage. The decision to move to Orlando is obvious when you factor in San Jose's housing shortage. While Americans used to move to prosperity, restrictive zoning perversely provides Americans with clear incentives to avoid those places where they could make the largest contributions to the economy.[21]

This has serious implications for the health of the US economy. As we discussed above, large and growing cities make us more productive, which is why they have historically been the setting for sustained economic growth.[22] By pricing Americans out of the largest labor markets, we prevent them from specializing, absorbing the wisdom of knowledge spillovers, or potentially starting new and innovative businesses. Beyond merely closing doors to Americans in distressed regions like Appalachia and the Mississippi Delta who might have moved to opportunity, zoning has thwarted the continued growth of our most productive regions.

This has resulted in some strange outcomes. Consider broader mobility patterns: all else being equal, we would expect people to move out of cities where incomes were low in 2010 and into cities where incomes were high. But consider where Americans have moved over the past decade. On the one hand, a few cities you would expect to shrink—such as Detroit or St. Louis, which sit at or below the national median income—did shrink between 2010 and 2020. And a few affluent cities—such as DC and Seattle, which posted median incomes well above the national figure—also grew by 1 to 2 percent each year.

Yet many of the the fastest-growing major cities over the past decade—including cities like Orlando, Fort Worth, Durham, Charlotte, and Omaha—were all essentially right at the national median. Indeed, in Orlando, one of the fastest growing cities over the past decade, median incomes in 2010 were actually around $3,000 below the national median. At the same time, many of our nation's wealthiest cities, largely clustered in California—San Diego, San Francisco, and San Jose—all grew at less than 1 percent per year. Los Angeles didn't even crack 3 percent population growth over the *entire decade*. This is an inversion of the historical norm of Americans moving to prosperity, and many economists agree that zoning-induced high housing costs are largely to blame. Why move to a more productive city if higher housing costs will eat up all of your additional income, and then some?

How Much Poorer Are We?

As a result of this strange inversion in American mobility, we are all poorer. But how much poorer? By misallocating so much of the US labor market, economists Chang-Tai Hsieh and Enrico Moretti put the annual loss in wages associated with zoning at around $1.6 trillion each year.[23] Hsieh and Moretti estimate that these policies reduced economic growth between 1964 and 2009 by 36 percent. They further estimate that relaxing zoning in New York City, San Francisco, and San Jose alone would have raised aggregate gross domestic product in 2009 by 9 percent. Reframed for 2020, that would mean that zoning in three cities is costing the US economy nearly $2 trillion. That's not exactly chump change.

A more recent paper by economists Gilles Duranton and Diego Puga using a different methodology suggests that this might even understate the foregone wealth caused by zoning.[24] Exploring what might happen if some of our largest and wealthiest cities liberalized zoning, their model suggests that output per person in a place like Boston would rise by just over 13 percent. The gains would be most pronounced for new arrivals, who would see real incomes rise by just over a quarter. In the aggregate, if our three most productive cities were to tame zoning, US real per capita income would rise by just over 8 percent. That's a lot of growth to turn down, even accounting for the costs that would come with scaling up cities like New York City and San Francisco.

By making it hard for Americans to move to prosperous cities, zoning may also be deepening regional inequality. Between 1880 and 1980, incomes among the Northeast, South, Mountain West, and Midwest were gradually converging, as working-class Americans in poorer regions packed up and departed for more prosperous cities. One famous example of this is the Great Migration of African Americans from the South to the North, but similar trends played among Dust Bowl "Okies" heading west during the Great Depression and Appalachians heading north and west during and after World War II. Beyond merely improving their station, this also helped to temper incomes in wealthier regions and raise incomes in poorer regions.

According to economists Peter Ganong and Daniel Shoag, this income convergence has mostly stalled since 1980, right around the time that American zoning started to tighten.[25] As we saw earlier, Americans are now more likely to move from wealthier regions to poorer regions than the other way around—whether from California to Arizona or from New York to Florida. Ganong and Shoag blame this peculiar inversion partly on housing costs, which gobble up whatever income gains would have been made by moving and making the move to more productive cities financially irrational. If we had merely allowed income convergence to continue—such as by avoiding zoning-induced housing shortages in cities like San Francisco and Boston—Ganong and Shoag estimate the national increase in wage inequality would have been 8 percent smaller between 1980 and 2010. In this sense, zoning not only makes us poorer but also more unequal.

⋅⋅▌⋅⋅

The problem of zoning raising housing costs isn't just a matter of high rents or expensive homes in a few select cities: by systematically blocking access to our most productive cities, zoning makes America a less innovative, less wealthy, more unequal place. Large, dense cities are the engines of American prosperity, spinning off the world's most productive firms and path-breaking innovations. To the extent that we are serious about successfully transitioning to an innovation-oriented economy, we must clear away barriers that are blocking cities from absorbing a lot more people. And that means critically reevaluating the way we regulate land.

Now more than ever, we need cities to grow.[26] Not for folks who are already wealthy, but for those still seeking opportunity. It isn't enough to *have* large innovative cities. We also need to ensure that they can accommodate everyone who might like to move and participate in the prosperity they offer. Growth is about more than flashier smartphones or faster food delivery—it's also about making it easy for a family in a down-and-out place like Eastern Kentucky or a shrinking Rust Belt town to move to a city where they can pursue the good life for themselves and their offspring. Stagnation is complicated. Inequality is messy. And abolishing zoning is hardly a silver bullet. But to the extent that we can clear a path for the small, courageous act of moving to opportunity, we have an obligation to remove that barrier.

CHAPTER 5
Apartheid by Another Name

Over the summer of 2020, the United States underwent a long-overdue reckoning in the aftermath of the murder of George Floyd at the hands of Minneapolis police officers. Across virtually every city in the country, an estimated fifteen to twenty-six million Americans protested the continued mistreatment of Blacks by the criminal justice system.[1] Whether the Black Lives Matter movement will translate into meaningful policy reform remains to be seen. If nothing else, the movement signals an encouraging willingness of many Americans to continue to right past injustices and build a more equitable republic.

And yet, for all the good intentions, America remains a profoundly segregated place. Indeed, this segregation—both of the class and racial varieties—is written into law by local zoning codes. Since zoning first took root in the early twentieth century, it has invariably been used to enforce and perpetuate a uniquely American form of apartheid, shrouded in a fog of planning jargon and obtuse codes. The same mechanisms that allow local governments to drive up local housing costs or prohibit affordable typologies give local governments the ability to decide who gets to live where, or if they are allowed in town at all. The victims have been the poor and marginalized, whom zoning has consistently shunted into neighborhoods and municipalities with the most environmental hazards and the worst public services.

While you will find no mention of race or class in your contemporary local zoning ordinances, the open pursuit of American apartheid forms the basis of many zoning codes still in effect today. Birmingham, Alabama—often dubbed America's Johannesburg, a nod to South Africa's notoriously segregated capital—imposed a system of explicit racial zoning through 1951. The modern civil rights movement, which fully flowered in Birmingham in the 1960s, can trace its roots in part to early efforts by Black residents to move into neighborhoods zoned exclusively for Whites, setting off a string of White-on-Black bombings that plagued the city through 1961. Birmingham was hardly alone: most southern cities at one point or another enforced explicitly racial zoning, at least through the first quarter of the twentieth century.

While the courts clamped down on de jure racial zoning in 1917, court approval of economic zoning in 1926 would pave the way for de facto racial segregation, pursued through zoning regulations designed to enshrine class segregation. Southern cities were quick to bring in renowned zoning framers who could provide legal cover for the same old exclusionary zoning codes. Drawing on local anti-Chinese sentiments, West Coast zoning would pursue similar aims, while prejudice against Jews, the Irish, and everyone in between would help to underwrite zoning's spread through the Northeast. When African Americans moved en masse to the West Coast and Northeast as part of the Great Migration, zoning codes in cities across the country were quick to adopt the lessons of southern segregationists.

Although uncouth references to race have been prudently papered over in contemporary codes, openly segregationist zoning codes remain in full legal force in most American cities. While historically associated

An "All Are Welcome" yard sign next to a yard sign opposing zoning liberalization in Austin, the irony apparently lost on the homeowner. (M. Nolan Gray)

with the South, exclusionary zoning can now be found in affluent neighborhoods across the country, including in self-styled progressive urban neighborhoods in places like Brooklyn or Austin. Through a witch's brew of tight density restrictions, sweeping prohibitions on apartments, and high minimum lot sizes, among other zoning regulations, these neighborhoods and suburbs effectively preserve their economic exclusivity and high-quality services to the detriment of everyone else.

Combined with other planning initiatives, zoning largely succeeded in preserving segregation where it existed and instituting segregation where it didn't. Indeed, one study finds that cities that adopted zoning between 1900 and 1930 exhibited significantly higher levels of racial and economic segregation in 1970, controlling for a host of potential confounding variables.[2] And while racial segregation has slightly moderated

since 1970—no thanks to zoning—class segregation has only continued to worsen, with this trend most pronounced in cities with the most
restrictive land-use regulations, zoning key among them. Combine this
segregation with unequal public service provision and the result is a system of zoning that methodically corrals the most vulnerable Americans
into the worst neighborhoods. This chapter explains how that system
came to be and how it continues to shape cities.

Zoning for Segregation

Before the federal government got involved, uptake of zoning was modest.
One exception to this was in southern states, where zoning offered a
powerful tool for reasserting strict segregation, which had slackened in
the aftermath of the Civil War but had gradually reemerged after the end
of Reconstruction in the 1880s. The South was hardly the first American
region to deploy land-use regulation toward segregationist ends—since
the 1880s, California cities had been battling with the courts to segregate
Chinese-owned businesses by way of earlier forms of zoning. But southern
cities would take this to the next level in the 1910s as early adopters of
zoning and, in so doing, would play a powerful role in shaping the institution that now governs cities nationwide.

The first racial zoning ordinance was adopted in Baltimore in 1910.
The ordinance restricted African Americans from buying homes on
majority White blocks, and vice versa, enforcing block-by-block segregation. In light of the surprisingly high level of residential integration
already present in Baltimore—particularly in less affluent districts—the
ordinance quickly proved to be unworkable, forcing regulators to switch
to a standard of restricting African American buyers only on *fully* White
blocks. A "Baptists and bootleggers" alliance of Progressive reformers
and racist homeowners would spread Baltimore-style racial zoning across
the South, including to major cities like Atlanta, Dallas, and Louisville.

LOOK At These Homes NOW!

An entire block ruined by negro invasion.   Every house marked "X" now occupied by negroes.   ACTUAL PHOTOGRAPH OF 4300 WEST BELLE PLACE.

SAVE YOUR HOME! VOTE FOR SEGREGATION!

 73

A flyer from the 1916 St. Louis campaign to adopt racial zoning. While this variety of explicitly racist zoning was quickly struck down by the Supreme Court, St. Louis had no trouble finding new ways of using zoning as a tool for segregation. (Missouri History Museum on Wikimedia.org)

In 1917, only one year after the first modern zoning ordinances went into effect in New York City and Berkeley, the Supreme Court would strike down Louisville's racial zoning ordinance in *Buchanan v. Warley*. While many major cities would continue to pursue explicitly racial zoning for decades through a blend of outright defiance and legal loopholes—Birmingham continued to enforce racial zoning until 1951—the fate of explicitly racial zoning was sealed in the courts.

The introduction of modern zoning in 1916, and subsequent promotion by the federal government, provided a new avenue for pursuing segregation.[3] While explicit mentions of race would not be tolerated by the courts, zoning actively assumed economic segregation, which had clear racial implications. Segregationists were quick to learn this lesson. In the aftermath of *Buchanan*, cities like Atlanta and New Orleans quickly hired renowned early planning consultants like Robert Whitten and Harland Bartholomew to provide a professional gloss—and hopefully legal cover—for de facto racial zoning, this time pursued through class segregation.[4]

Southern cities used zoning to perpetuate racial segregation in two general ways. On the one hand, White neighborhoods were downzoned, such that affordable housing could not be built. That is to say, homes couldn't be subdivided into small apartment buildings, larger lots couldn't be divided up into smaller lots, and new apartments were prohibited.[5] Such neighborhoods were generally in the most favorable locations, free of environmental hazards and with access to quality public services. On the other hand, affordable housing typologies, particularly apartments, were exclusively zoned in neighborhoods that were already poor and majority African American. These zones were regularly mapped in areas with significant environmental risks, adjacent to hazardous industrial districts, and with extremely poor public services, often altogether lacking sewerage.[6]

By allowing White homeowners to decide who could live where, zoning formed the bedrock of planning for segregation. But it was only the tip of the iceberg. As urban planning professor Charles Connerly recounts in his sweeping history of the planning of Birmingham, zoning was guided by comprehensive plans explicit in identifying White areas and Black areas, with public service provision focused on the former and denied to the latter.[7] Indeed, official planning documents in cities like Austin and Kansas City continued to refer to "Black neighborhoods" and "White neighborhoods" as late as the 1980s.[8] Public housing, which was segregated until 1954, would strengthen the patterns of segregation instituted by zoning, as would federal highway construction, which was often used to buffer White areas from Black areas. Where Black neighborhoods managed to survive against these extreme headwinds, urban renewal—or as James Baldwin characterized it, "negro removal"— would erase poor neighborhoods altogether, with Black neighborhoods in particular in the crosshairs.

As African Americans moved north and west en masse as part of the Great Migration that surrounded the First and Second World Wars, the practice of strictly downzoning affluent White residential areas while relegating affordable housing to the worst parts of town would also spread, stripping the poor of their right to move to opportunity. Indianapolis would try its hand at explicitly racial zoning in 1926, and the use of planning powers—key among them, zoning—to segregate poor residents into subpar neighborhoods was well under way in cities like Los Angeles and Chicago by the middle of the twentieth century.

The national spread of exclusionary zoning was backed in no small part by federal housing policy, which sought to perpetuate racial segregation. As legal scholar Richard Rothstein explains, the dominant role that the government played in housing markets beginning with the New Deal would serve to aggressively promote racial segregation. By setting federal underwriting standards, key agencies like the Federal Housing Administration (FHA) could dictate the behavior of local governments, developers, and prospective homeowners.[9]

Federally backed mortgages came with a clear expectation of strict racial and class segregation, essentially requiring the local adoption of conventional zoning, with its strict separation of uses and tight restrictions on density. At the same time, such standards cut off financing to the urban neighborhoods that African Americans called home, through a policy now known as redlining. While many of these explicitly segregationist housing finance policies have been phased out, the resulting patterns of racial segregation and extreme racial inequality in housing wealth remain to this day. The zoning laws that underwrote this system remain on the books in nearly every major US city.

All Are Welcome, If You Can Afford It

If the story ended here, the case against zoning would be weak. After all, what public policy wasn't drafted into the cause of racial segregation at one point or another? If the use of zoning toward segregationist ends were merely historical, there would be no more of a case for scrapping zoning than there would be for scrapping road construction or public schools. The trouble is that zoning remains first and foremost a tool of racial and economic exclusion. So long as even a tiny minority of homeowners associate racial or economic homogeneity with high property values, or would prefer to keep exclusive access to jobs and high-quality public services to themselves, zoning will always function as a tool of segregation.[10]

In the aftermath of the civil rights movement, the exclusive hold that White homeowners had over the city ended. With it went part of their power to use zoning to maintain racial and economic segregation within the city, which had in turn been used to keep public schools segregated by race and class. In response, as political scientist Jessica Trounstine recounts, White homeowners increasingly retreated to separately incorporated suburbs, where they could resume their hold over zoning and public service allocation. As a result, while racial segregation has notably declined *within* cities since 1970, it has virtually remained flat *among* cities.[11]

The fact is, many affluent neighborhoods and suburbs continue to use zoning to perpetuate patterns of segregation in the same way they use zoning to raise housing costs. Through regulations like large minimum lot sizes, apartment bans, or restrictions on manufactured housing, communities often weaponize zoning to keep the poor out of those neighborhoods and suburbs with the best access to jobs or highest quality schools. Though the courts have taken a dim view of racial zoning, they have long tolerated economic zoning, beginning with Justice

Sutherland's characterization of apartments as "mere parasite[s]" in the case that deemed zoning constitutional.[12]

Despite its southern origins, exclusionary zoning is now a nationwide phenomenon. Indeed, it's now at its worst in self-styled progressive regions like the Northeast or the West Coast. Tellingly, Trounstine begins her sweeping book on the intersection of planning and segregation not with Birmingham or Atlanta but with Philadelphia's New Jersey suburbs.[13] In the aftermath of World War II, with new federal highways and generous federal housing subsidies on offer, affluent White homeowners in Camden decamped for once-rural Cherry Hill and quickly threw up zoning barriers in their wake to keep the poor from following. The result was a degree of inequality so shocking, with such dramatic variation in public service quality, that New Jersey courts were eventually forced to act. The result was the famous Mount Laurel doctrine, which requires each municipality to permit its fair share of housing.[14]

The poor in other states haven't been so lucky. In the notoriously exclusionary Connecticut suburbs of New York City, for example, developers seeking to build affordable housing—such as townhomes or small apartment buildings—are often embarking on a suicide mission. As documented by journalist Lisa Prevost in her intimate portrait of exclusionary planning in New England, zoning allows municipalities to pursue racial and economic segregation without mentioning race or class at all.[15] Simply by setting astronomically high minimum lot sizes or banning apartments, wealthy suburbs and towns can block the construction of most kinds of affordable housing.

As Prevost documents in the case of Darien, Connecticut, any developer foolish enough to apply for a variance or rezoning to build affordable housing will face years of process and dozens of public hearings.[16] The developer—not infrequently a nonprofit, as this process virtually never makes business sense—will be impugned as a greedy usurper. Studies will be mandated based on unfounded environmental concerns.

Unrepresentative speakers will deploy coded language about preserving community character.[17] And even if the occasional project can survive such a process, it will only ever be too little, too late to make a dent in the segregated patterns of living we inherited from a less enlightened age.

The Bitter Fruits of Segregation

Originally devised to perpetuate segregation where it already existed and introduce segregation where it didn't, zoning has been remarkably successful on its terms, to the detriment of building a fairer society. Between 1900 and 1940, a pivotal period for zoning adoption, racial and economic segregation increased by a startling 50 percent in US cities.[18] Segregation would continue to worsen through the postwar suburban building boom up until 1970, by which point federal legislation and an active court finally began to crack down on racial segregation.

Zoning was hardly alone in perpetuating these trends, helped along as it was by prejudiced homeowners, restrictive racial covenants, and a raft of federal interventions designed to segregate American life. But thanks to additional analyses by Trounstine, we know that zoning played an important role. Consider the differences between early and late adopters of zoning. In 1900, cities that would go on to be enthusiastic early adopters of zoning had slightly less racial segregation than those that would hold out on zoning. But by 1970, cities that had adopted zoning before 1930 exhibited rates of segregation over 25 percent higher than cities that would adopt zoning later, even controlling for various potentially confounding factors.[19]

Thanks to recent research in this space, we know with some certainty which specific zoning rules drive racial segregation. According to one paper, increasing the zoned density of an area by one unit per acre is associated with a 0.50 percent increase in Hispanics and a 0.38 percent increase in Blacks as a percentage of the population.[20] This effect is even more pronounced with use regulation: simply allowing apartments on a block—rare in most zoned cities—is associated with a 5.77 percent increase in the local Hispanic population and a 3.36 percent increase in the local Black population. All this is to say, by banning smaller units and rentals, zoning continues to serve its original purpose of perpetuating racial segregation.

Indeed, similar trends can increasingly be observed in renter segregation—a useful proxy for economic segregation—which increased at *twice* the rate among early zoning adopters. While racial segregation has slightly abated thanks to robust federal policy interventions, economic segregation has only deepened over the past half century. One study by urban planning professors Michael C. Lens and Paavo Monkkonen, which surveyed the link between land-use regulation and segregation across ninety-five metropolitan areas, finds that zoning continues to play a driving role in keeping rich and poor separate.[21] It does so, the authors find, by allowing the wealthiest parts of town to wall themselves off.

The combined result is that zoning reserves the best parts of every town for an elite few—not only the best housing, but also often the best school districts, the best public services, and the best access to jobs. And it shows up in the data, with basic quality of life metrics like life expectancy, lifetime earnings, and educational attainment varying dramatically from neighborhood to neighborhood and suburb to suburb.[22] Zoning systematically locks our most vulnerable populations out of those neighborhoods and suburbs where they would be best positioned to find opportunity, both for themselves and for their children. If we are serious about tackling inequality, we must critically reevaluate the way we regulate land.

॥▮॥

On its face, the persistence of segregation is a puzzle. While race relations are hardly perfect, prejudice has declined markedly over the past half century, such that once divisive questions like "Do you approve or disapprove of Whites and Blacks living near one another?" have fallen off of surveys altogether.[23] With near-unanimous approval, it simply isn't an interesting question to ask. The same is true of class prejudice, which has never found firm footing on North American soil: there is wide agreement among Americans on ensuring equality of opportunity.[24] Better yet, there is wide agreement that we have a shared social obligation to ensure that everyone has access to decent housing.[25] And yet, racial segregation at the metropolitan level has virtually remained flat since 1970, while economic segregation has worsened. What gives?

The missing piece to this puzzle is zoning. The reality is that, regardless of changing prejudices or preferences, our cities and suburbs remain under the shadow of a system of land-use regulation carefully calibrated to maintain racial and economic segregation. Far from merely rationalizing land uses or prudently managing densities, the heart of your local zoning code was more likely than not written with the express intention of separating rich from poor and, depending on your local history, White from Black, Anglo from Latino, European from Asian. We do our society no favors by pulling punches on this fact: zoning is a tool of segregation.

CHAPTER 6

Sprawl by Design

On a warm late-summer evening in Queens, roughly a hundred locals had shown up for the monthly meeting of their neighborhood community board. Hosted in a local community center, the air was stuffy and the mood almost sleepy. As a city planner, it was my job to represent the city at these community board hearings, which had been tasked with reviewing land-use applications since 1975. On the heels of urban renewal, the city understandably opted to let locals have a say in developments that required extra zoning approvals. The snag was that as the zoning became tighter, more and more run-of-the-mill development projects would get swept up in the increasingly raucous public review process.

The project at that night's meeting was one such vanilla project. The proposal called for the conversion of an old hospital building—which had been shuttered since the Great Recession—into apartments and the construction of a new fourteen-story residential building on the back half of the lot. From a planning perspective, it was a slam dunk. The disused hospital building, once an eyesore, would now host medical office space on the ground floor and approximately 140 income-restricted units for seniors—two pressing needs in the aging community. The new fourteen-story apartment building would add approximately 220 new apartments to one of the most expensive neighborhoods in Queens. To top it all off, the proposed development site was less than a quarter mile from a subway stop and a major shopping district, meaning that most residents could comfortably live without a car.

The trouble was that the project site was in a zoning district where nothing more than single-family housing is allowed, so the developer needed to apply for a rezoning, which involved seeking the blessing of the local community board. As a young planner, I naively assumed the project would sail through. There were the typical unrelated concerns about flooding, school overcrowding, and traffic, as you might expect. The developer's attorney, hardly new to the game, had answers for the common complaints down pat. But as things were wrapping up, a local activist stood up to make a kind of environmental case against the new apartments: "At a certain point, we have to ask: How much growth is enough? How much more burden can we put on our environment? Not all growth is good, you know. Cancer is a growth."

Without a clear ask from the speaker, the attorney understandably disregarded the outburst. And moved by the prospect of subsidized units for people like them, the senior-dominated board was already sold on the project. Assurances to build fewer family-sized units and to build additional parking would allay any lingering doubt. But the activist tapped into a sentiment you hear often in public hearings: the idea that growing cities are a threat to the environment. In one sense, it makes sense: cities are a completely artificial construct and, worse yet, they are noisy, smelly, and dirty.[1] Surely they are terrible for the environment, right?

Just the opposite—while environmentalists have historically envisaged a rustic cabin in the mountains as the green ideal, New York may just be the greenest major settlement in America. As David Owen points out in *Green Metropolis*, New Yorkers consume far less energy, gasoline, and land per resident while producing less in the way of pollution, trash, and greenhouse gas emissions than their suburban peers.[2] If everyone in the borough of Manhattan alone were forced to live at the density of Oklahoma City—one of America's least dense major cities—it would take up roughly 1,600 square miles of land, an area approximately the size of Delaware. As all those apartment dwellers and transit riders bought McMansions and cars, gasoline and electricity consumption would nearly double, along with attendant increases in emissions and air pollution.

If this hypothetical transformation of urban form happened in one instant, it would be appropriately recognized as one of the worst environmental catastrophes in US history. Yet zoning perpetuates this crisis in millions of small ways every day, invisible to the casual observer. By forcing cities to sprawl out, writing automobile dependence into law, and pricing Americans out of our most temperate cities, zoning is a slow-motion environmental disaster and deserves to be recognized as such. If we are serious about preserving undeveloped land, reducing our fossil fuel dependence, and lowering greenhouse gas emissions, zoning has to go.

Zoning for Sprawl

For many in my generation, hating on sprawl was a kind of gateway drug into thinking about cities. For a coming-of-age teenager, the seemingly endless series of near-identical strip malls and tract homes that make up suburbia can be an alienating and ugly place. Nourished by films like *American Beauty*, albums like Arcade Fire's *The Suburbs*, and the razor-sharp prose of suburban critics like James Howard Kunstler, society does little to dissuade us from this anti-suburban impulse.[3] And there's a lot to criticize, even beyond superficial concerns about aesthetics: new growth on the periphery often gobbles up wilderness, and all the infrastructure it takes to maintain sprawl certainly doesn't come cheap.[4]

In this regard, the environmental pitch for cities is straightforward: they simply take up less space. Indeed, the most obvious way that cities reduce our impact on the Earth is by allowing us to economize on land. Despite being home to two out of every three Americans, cities only take up 3.5 percent of the land.[5] By building up, cities reduce the need to build out, which would normally mean building out onto meadows, forests, deserts, and wetlands. As hundreds of millions of people have poured into cities over the past few decades—particularly in the developing world—this has been an unambiguous win for the environment, allowing millions of acres of land to return to wilderness.[6]

Beyond economizing on land, cities also improve energy efficiency: living in a smaller townhouse or an apartment—a decision often made for urban residents by higher housing costs—can dramatically reduce electricity consumption. By one estimate, a household in a detached single-family house consumes three times as much energy as a household in an apartment.[7] This difference mostly comes down to the cost of heating and cooling, which alone accounts for half of a household's residential energy consumption. Apartments are more energy efficient in part because of their shared walls and in part because they generally take up less space, both of which make climate control easier. According to the US Energy Information Administration, apartments have only grown more energy efficient over the past five decades. Over the same period, energy efficiency has slightly worsened among detached single-family homes, mainly owing to their increasing size.[8] By letting cities build up rather than out, we save not only land but also energy.

This isn't to say that *all* sprawl is bad. At least *some* suburban growth is natural and, dare I say, even desirable. As architectural historian Robert Bruegmann points out, cities and towns have grown outward since the dawn of time, across various cultural and topographical contexts.[9] As populations and economies incrementally grow, cities naturally consume more space. Likewise, as incomes increase, folks find that they would like—and can afford—larger homes on larger parcels. In recent centuries these natural trends have been emboldened by improvements in transportation technologies that make getting into and out of the city each day a little easier. Today, we tend to associate this with cars. But in their day, technologies like horse-drawn omnibuses and streetcars also drove sprawl.

What most people likely have in mind when they complain about sprawl is *excessive* urban growth on the periphery. If we were encouraging cities to take up more land than they might otherwise require, that would certainly be a problem. As urban economist Jan Brueckner notes, public policy does exactly that, encouraging excessive sprawl in a host of ways: few US cities price the social costs with lost open space, congestion, or new infrastructure correctly, giving a free pass to sprawl developers and residents to impose costs on the rest of society. Addressing any of these issues is worth the time of policymakers and planners. But even if we got the prices right, this would leave out one of the major drivers of sprawl in America: zoning.

As we briefly discussed in chapter 1, the framers of zoning saw their purpose as reducing urban densities by spreading cities out. Early planners were heavily inspired by an urban design ideal of detached single-family homes on large lots, flanked by expansive yards. Pioneered by mid-nineteenth-century suburban developments like Riverside, Illinois—designed by then-starchitects Frederick Law Olmsted and Calvert Vaux—planners envisioned a romantic, pastoralist pattern of development, shrouded in rhetoric about returning man to nature.[10] It was a message perfectly optimized to appeal to an American environmentalist tradition steeped in the thinking of rural hermits like Henry David Thoreau and John Muir.

The results have been decidedly less romantic. In practice, this century-long vision of suppressing densities and blending the city and countryside through zoning has effectively mandated a landscape of sprawling subdivisions and strip malls—a far cry from the leafy suburban demonstration

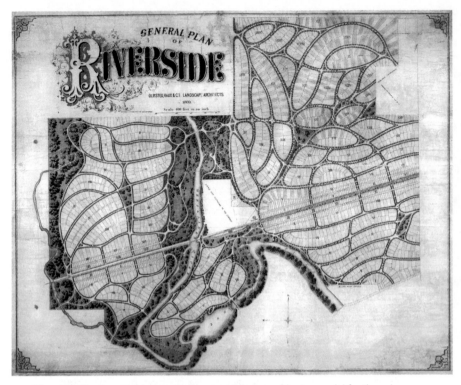

Riverside, Illinois: a pioneering development that would set a model for the urban design of modern suburbia. (Village of Riverside, Illinois)

projects of the late 1800s. The zoning that emerged from this frame-work has been an environmental disaster for a lot of reasons. It assumes universal car ownership and prohibits efficient apartment living. But it also just plain wastes space: if you didn't know any better, you might be forgiven for thinking that your local zoning ordinance was carefully cali-brated to use up as much land as possible.

We have already discussed some of these policies: minimum lot size regulations, for example, force lots for single-family homes to be larger than they otherwise might have been. Lacking any clear health or safety justification, these rules do little more than raise housing costs and force each house to take up more land, driving sprawl farther into

The ultimate zoned landscape: Levittown, Pennsylvania, circa 1959. A decidedly less romantic outcome than Riverside. (The College of New Jersey on Wikimedia.org)

the countryside. Or take single-family zoning, which makes it illegal to build apartments in vast swaths of most US cities. By mandate of zoning, a lot of housing that might have been built as green downtown apartments instead ends up being built as brown detached homes out on the edge of town.

But consider also setbacks: these rules force buildings to sit a certain distance back from the property line, with the land in between remaining unused. In a typical single-family zoning district, the rules usually call for something like a 20-foot front setback, 8-foot side setbacks, and a 30-foot rear setback.[11] On a typical 5,000 square foot lot, this leaves only 2,100 square feet for the building envelope, leaving 58 percent of the lot unused as a matter of law. Many zoning codes double down on this waste with separate regulations, such as maximum lot coverage rules or minimum open space rules, which typically force 70 to 75 percent of every lot to go to waste.

Much of this wasted land ends up as lawns surrounding homes or landscaped strips on the periphery of strip malls or, worse yet, simply paved over for parking. In such unnatural settings, we witness the down-stream results of zoning's attempt to blend city and nature by regulatory fiat: largely ignored spaces which in turn hurt the environment to the extent that they require water, chemical fertilizers, and weed killers, as well as regular, fuel-intensive mowing and maintenance.[12] By one esti-mate, this throwaway landscape of crabgrass and dwarf hollies has now become our number one irrigated crop.[13]

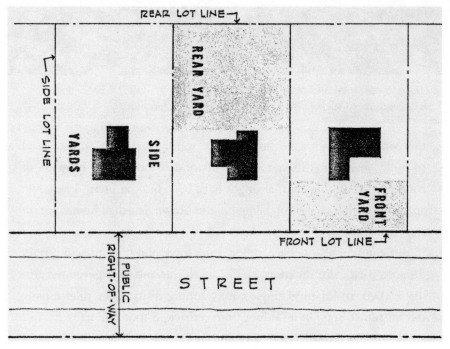

A 1962 illustration of the setback rules that would come to define the American suburban landscape. (Port Huron-St. Clair County Planning)

If planners simply set aside space for public parks and allowed private land to be used to its fullest potential, they might save genuine nature from being developed out on the periphery. Instead, zoning is designed to engineer the worst of both worlds: cities turn into an unpleasant archipelago of isolated, energy-intensive buildings standing amid a sea of surface lots, lawns, and minimally compliant shrubbery. Meanwhile, the countryside devolves into a rigidly patterned landscape of subdivisions and malls, forced to accommodate all the growth that zoning has locked out of the city. A dense city may not look green to the untrained eye, but consider that every urban apartment, office, or storefront masks a patch of wilderness on the periphery that need not be developed.

Assume a Car

Where we live can have an incredible impact on how we get around. Take my family history. Where my mom grew up, it would take a 26-mile car ride among the sigogglin country roads of Appalachia to get from her home at the head of a holler to the nearest full-service supermarket. Where I grew up, it would take a 2.3-mile car ride through thick Lexington suburbia to get from my parents' home to the nearest supermarket. Where I lived throughout 2020, in downtown Washington, DC, it took a half-mile walk along an active street grid to get to a supermarket, assuming the half dozen or so bodegas and corner groceries along the way didn't have what I needed.

Healthy cities naturally gravitate toward greater density and use mixture over time. As more people jockey to be in the same place, whether to live or to work, they bid up the price of land, providing developers with an incentive to economize on land by building up. Before zoning, this meant apartments and offices springing up over shops and single-family homes converting into small apartment buildings. Where this is still allowed, this gradual rise in density and increasing mixture of uses in turn reshapes how we move around the city.

For starters, trips get shorter. This works at all density scales: while the suburbs of Lexington, with a population density of 1,043 residents per square mile, are no one's idea of an urban utopia—walking to that supermarket would be a perilous hour-long journey along ditches and freeways—it's still far easier to get around than in an Appalachian hamlet, which has a population density of 56 residents per square mile. A similar scaling effect occurs even within built-out cities, particularly for goods and services, as larger markets can support more of both. In Washington, DC, with a population density of 11,506 residents per square mile, the supermarket is a short walk away; back where I lived in Manhattan, with its population density of 69,468 residents per square mile, the supermarket was literally on my block.[14]

As a side effect of this density, cities naturally produce environments that give residents choice about how to get around, including the option to get around without harming the environment. As densities rise, urban residents begin to enjoy the choice to use means other than cars to get around, whether by foot, bicycle, or transit. Take gasoline consumption, which makes up about one-fifth of US energy consumption. As Owen notes, the typical resident of Vermont—renowned for its commitment to environmentalist causes—consumes three and a half times as much gasoline per year as the typical resident of New York City.[15] Narrow it down to the most densely built part of the city—Manhattan—and Vermonters use *six* times as much gasoline.

One estimate by economists Edward Glaeser and Matthew Kahn suggests that a resident of an area with a population density of fewer than one thousand residents per square mile consumes nearly twice as much gasoline as a resident in an area with over ten thousand residents per square mile.[16] That means that within a single metropolitan area, annual gasoline consumption might fall by three hundred gallons as you move from a suburb to an urban area. All of this is to say, by reducing distances and increasing densities, cities *substantially* reduce our carbon footprint.

And this seems to work in a superlinear fashion: as a city doubles in population density, Glaeser and Kahn find that carbon emissions per household fall by one ton.

By forbidding density, zoning makes this shift away from the car difficult. The literature varies widely on this issue, but there is a reasonable consensus among transportation planners that a city needs densities of at least seven dwelling units per acre to support the absolute baseline of transit: a bus that stops every thirty minutes. To get more reliable service, like bus rapid transit or light-rail service, a city needs just over double those densities, or approximately fifteen units per acre.[17] The standard detached single-family residential district—which forms the basis of zoning and remains mapped in the vast majority of most cities—supports a maximum density of approximately five dwelling units per acre.[18] That is to say, zoning makes efficient transit effectively illegal in large swaths of our cities, to say nothing of our suburbs.

Worse yet, zoning often thwarts transit where it already exists, squandering taxpayer investments in transit—by blocking potential riders—and forcing more Americans into auto-oriented developments. And it seems to do so against the wishes of many residents and employers. As urban planner Jonathan Levine observes, demand to locate in and adjacent to transit is quite high among many Americans, as reflected by high land prices in those areas.[19] Economists Emily Hamilton and Eli Dourado pick up on similar land value premiums in walkable areas.[20] Yet zoning often ignores this demand, capping densities in precisely the places where many aspirational car-free commuters might like to live.[21] If people want to live in a way that dramatically reduces the impact of their commute on the environment—and developers are eager to build this housing for them—why would we stop this?

Beyond suppressing density, the other half of zoning—use zoning—might play an even greater role in lengthening vehicle trips and undermining the ability to walk, bicycle, or take transit. When people have the option to live near where they work and shop, they often choose to do so. On the flip side, when certain types of businesses have the option to locate near customers, they often do. Historically, it was the norm for even low-density residential neighborhoods to host corner groceries, barbershops, and doctors' offices, making daily chores on foot a breeze. Today, such a development pattern is almost universally illegal due to zoning, forcing even the most humdrum trips to involve a car.

Then there is parking: standard zoning rules frequently force developers to build at least one or two parking spaces per residential unit. In this regard, zoning assumes that every resident owns a car, which may not be the case in many walkable or transit-accessible neighborhoods. And once a unit is built with a parking spot and the resident has already been forced to eat the cost, why not just buy a car?[22] After all, most zoning

Across DC, you may see houses that look conspicuously like storefronts. Before zoning, use mixture of this sort was common. But since the adoption of zoning, these shops and offices have been forced out of residential neighborhoods, making cities less walkable and dynamic. (M. Nolan Gray)

codes will also force any location they might travel to—from shops to offices to bars—to also provide off-street parking. This will usually come in the form of a massive surface lot, which has the added effect of reducing densities and making walking profoundly unpleasant. In this way, zoning simultaneously forces us to collectively subsidize driving while making walking, bicycling, and taking transit as uncomfortable as possible.

From top to bottom, zoning undermines two of the great advantages of living in a city: shorter, less stressful commutes, and choice in how we get around. By suppressing densities, segregating uses, and mandating abundant free parking, zoning effectively forces most urban residents to own a car and spend a lot of time driving to work or making endless errand runs. As normal as the resulting addiction to gasoline may seem today—after a century of letting zoning reshape our cities—it doesn't have to be this way. If an American wants to live a greener life and scrap their car, why should zoning stand in the way?

Fleeing Sustainability

As a result of high housing costs—an issue we discussed in chapter 3—Americans have spent the past decade streaming out of wealthy coastal cities like San Jose, Boston, and Los Angeles and into less affluent Sun Belt and Mountain West cities like Tampa, San Antonio, and Phoenix. An unknown number of people might like to live in the former category of cities but are forced to settle in the latter category of cities merely to find decent housing. This recent trend inverts the historical norm of Americans moving from poor areas to rich areas and leaves our country poorer and less innovative as a result.

In the same way that these zoning-related migration trends are stunting US economic growth, they're also making our country less green. Consider one of the worst offenders in terms of which regions are refusing to build more housing, coastal California. It's one of the greenest regions in the country in terms of household carbon emissions.[23] And this isn't because Californians take transit or live in apartments at particularly high rates—on the contrary. It's because California's famously temperate climate minimizes the need for energy-intensive climate control, which as we noted above, accounts for more than half of residential energy consumption. As a result, every single one of California's major cities—Los Angeles, San Diego, San Francisco, San Jose, and Sacramento—finds itself among the fifteen most energy-efficient cities in the country.[24]

Now consider the inverse, those cities building the most housing and accommodating the most population growth. Over the past decade, the six fastest-growing major cities were all in the Sun Belt, easily the brownest region in the US in terms of household carbon emissions.[25] Particularly in the Southeast, with hot summers and cool winters, there are few times in the year where either the AC or the heat isn't cranked up.[26] This shows up in electricity usage: Phoenix, San Antonio, and Dallas hold the dubious distinction of being among both the top five fastest-growing major cities *and* the top five energy consumers. Even if we could wave a magic wand and get every resident of these cities riding transit and living in apartments, they would still be far browner than their West Coast peers.

How is an environmentalist to respond to this conundrum? They could simply hope that new technologies might make living in the deserts of Arizona, the rolling hills of Texas, or the marshes of Florida less environmentally taxing. Indeed, low-cost electric vehicles and expanding renewable energy could all ease the burden in the years to come. But why hold out hope for some future fix when green cities already exist? Simply clearing away the zoning that drives up housing costs in places like San Francisco and San Diego is a zero-cost way to allow millions of Americans to voluntarily minimize their impact on the environment *today*. What are we waiting on?

'|█|'

Not everyone wants to live in an apartment, or a walkable neighborhood, or along the coasts, and that's okay. But a lot of people do. Left unmolested by misguided zoning policies, cities naturally tend toward greener patterns of development as densities incrementally rise, uses casually mix, and walking, bicycling, and taking transit become feasible. This is especially true of our greenest cities along the California coast, where millions of Americans would choose to live if given the choice. Why do we stop them?

Consider again the Queens story at the start of this chapter. In this case, a developer came to the city pleading for permission to build 351 apartments on an already-developed lot in one of the most walkable and transit-friendly neighborhoods in the country. From an environmental perspective, the project was a no-brainer: in addition to all the energy efficiency gains associated with apartments, these new units would be in an area where few residents would need to drive a car if they didn't want to.

For all New York City's tough talk about being a leader on climate change, zoning forced the developer behind this inherently green project to undertake the onerous process of pursuing a rezoning. This meant spending many thousands of dollars putting together an application, completing a nearly two-hundred-page environmental review, and getting grilled at no fewer than four public hearings. Yet if the developer had just relented and built what was allowed—eight detached single-family homes with lots of off-street parking—they could have pulled permits without any trouble at all.

Scale this all-too-typical zoning case up a few thousand times, and you can perhaps see why our cities are so sprawling and auto oriented. It might go without saying, but this is not sustainable. As with housing affordability, economic stagnation, and racial segregation, this is a crisis purely of our own making. But it doesn't have to be this way. In the next and final section of this book, we discuss how we can do better, whether by dramatically liberalizing zoning or moving past it altogether.

Part III

CHAPTER 7

Toward a Less Bad Zoning

The picture that this book has painted might seem bleak. Not without good reason: thanks in no small measure to zoning, millions of Americans struggle to make rent or mortgage payments. Worse yet, by locking so many Americans out of our most creative cities, we are collectively less productive and innovative. Meanwhile, zoning stands in the way of addressing the great issues of our time: for all the progress made in past decades, our cities are still shockingly segregated, along both racial and economic lines. And one of the most powerful tools we have for combating climate change—building more walkable, energy-efficient, compact cities—is blocked off by zoning codes adopted nearly a century ago.

The good news is that the tide is turning, as a steady trickle of zoning critiques have turned into a tidal wave of interest in reforming zoning. Thanks to an ideologically diverse coalition of pro-housing YIMBY (Yes In My Backyard) activists, pro-growth developers, antisegregation progressives, and environmentally minded urbanists, zoning reform has unexpectedly emerged as a cause célèbre. Across the country, a diverse array of cities and towns are gradually chipping away at the mainstays of zoning. Indeed, the most indefensible zoning policies, like single-family zoning and minimum parking requirements, are under fire like never before, and rightly so.

Even beyond the traditional home of city planning—local government—zoning reform is in the air. At the state level, strange bedfellows like Arkansas and Oregon are looking to rein in the powers of local government to block growth through zoning, with the former preempting minimum floor area requirements and the latter taking on excessive minimum lot sizes statewide. At the federal level, the push to reverse decades of federal support for exclusionary zoning now enjoys bipartisan support, as bills with unsubtle names like the Yes In My Backyard Act and the Build More Housing Near Transit Act wind their way through the US Congress.

Once the definitive local issue, American urbanists increasingly look abroad for what a fundamentally different zoning system might look like. What could the US possibly learn about zoning from a country as different from ours as Japan? Quite a lot. By setting district parameters at the national level, Japan limits the potential for local governments to adopt purely exclusionary use and density rules, with regional and national objectives driving zoning instead of local whims. The result is a zoning system that is exceptionally liberal by US standards, with far less use segregation and a more flexible attitude toward density. Making American zoning ever so slightly more like Japan's system would be a marked improvement.

Upcoming chapters will make the case for abolition and explore what land-use planning might look like after zoning. But with zoning as entrenched as it is today, abolition will be a heavy lift. At least over the next few years, we will be doing well to simply make zoning *less bad*. In light of this reality, this chapter sets out the "low-hanging fruit" of local zoning reform, considers the appropriate role of state and federal policymakers in driving reform, and briefly surveys what the US might learn from zoning abroad.

The Low-Hanging Fruit of Local Reform

For better or worse, local governments now determine most zoning policy in the US. While states and the federal government have an important role to play, local governments are nonetheless best positioned to reform zoning today. There are at least four zoning reforms that cities and suburbs must embrace: ending single-family zoning, abolishing minimum parking requirements, eliminating or lowering minimum floor area and minimum lot size requirements, and decriminalizing inherently affordable housing typologies. Let's dig into each of these reforms in turn.

END SINGLE-FAMILY ZONING

Single-family zoning forbids the construction of anything more than a detached single-family house on any given lot, such that duplexes, fourplexes, and larger apartment buildings are outright banned, a theme we discussed back in chapter 3. In a typical US city, at least three-quarters of the land zoned for residential uses will be zoned exclusively for single-family houses. In suburbs, this share can easily rise to 100 percent, allowing municipalities to effectively ban one of the most affordable forms of housing.

Needless to say, single-family zoning is a major hurdle to new affordable housing construction, as density is how less affluent residents outbid the rich for land. Imagine you own a four-thousand-square-foot house. You have two potential buyers: the first buyer intends to occupy it as a single-family house and can afford to pay $300,000. The second buyer intends to subdivide the home into four one-thousand-square-foot units renting at a modest market rate of $500 each. Assuming standard expenses and a 6 percent cap rate, this second buyer can afford to pay you $336,000. Who do you sell to? You don't need to be a bleeding-heart housing activist to go with the option that will entail more affordable housing.

Before zoning, this process of incremental housing growth played out over and over again in every American city. Single-family houses weren't the final word, as they are under zoning, but merely the first step. As demand grew, houses were divided into duplexes and fourplexes, turning mansions into apartments. By economizing on land and putting more housing units on the same plot, even working-class Americans were able to outbid the wealthy for mansions, thereby incrementally increasing the housing supply. Yet under zoning, creating this type of low-rise multi-family housing—often within walking distance of transit and commercial uses—is nearly always illegal.

As mentioned earlier, not every city is sitting on its hands when it comes to single-family zoning. In 2018, Minneapolis became the first city to abolish single-family zoning.[1] Like many American cities, Minneapolis had until recently zoned 70 percent of its land exclusively for single-family housing, with disastrous downstream implications for housing affordability and racial and economic segregation. Under the leadership of councilmember Lisa Bender and with support from Neighbors for More Neighbors, a local YIMBY group, the Minneapolis City Council voted twelve to one to abolish single-family zoning as part of its 2040 comprehensive plan overhaul, which by Minnesota law triggers associated changes in the zoning code. Duplexes and triplexes are now allowed in residential areas citywide.

Another tactic that cities have taken in phasing out single-family zoning has been to adopt liberal accessory dwelling unit (ADU) ordinances. Though single-family districts may remain on the zoning map, a liberal ADU ordinance offers a backdoor way to eliminate single-family zoning, namely by allowing extra housing units to go in the unused bedrooms, basements, attics, and garages of single-family houses. Cheap and easy to build, ADUs offer a politically expedient way to create inherently affordable housing in what are often affluent neighborhoods. As a side benefit, ADUs also allow homeowners to earn additional income by subdividing their homes and collecting rent.

An accessory dwelling unit (ADU) located in what was once likely an accessory garage. (Sightline Institute)

A testament to their salience as a political compromise for adding new housing in existing single-family neighborhoods, ADU ordinances have grown in popularity across the country, with ordinances sprouting up in cities as diverse as Somerville, Massachusetts, and Gainesville, Florida.[2] But getting the rules right is important: in many cases, cities adopt excessively strict rules surrounding ADUs, resulting in few units being built.

In 2018, Fayetteville, Arkansas, recognized as much when it amended its ADU ordinance to scrap an ADU owner-occupancy requirement—which required that property owners live in the primary unit—and eliminated the off-street parking requirements for new units, among other reforms.[3] At the same time, the city changed the rules to now allow one attached ADU and one interior ADU on every residential lot, such that Fayetteville now effectively enjoys citywide triplex zoning. While not as sexy as outright abolishing single-family zoning, the spread of ADUs constitutes meaningful progress.

ABOLISH MINIMUM PARKING REGULATIONS

Another necessary reform is the elimination of minimum parking require-ments, a theme we discussed back in chapter 6. These rules stipulate that for every so many residential units or square feet of commercial or industrial use a developer builds, they must also build so many off-street parking spaces. Cities initially adopted these rules to deal with the high demand for on-street parking. But these rules have many harmful side effects. For starters, they increase housing costs by forcing developers to build surface lots or parking garages, which require a lot of additional land and capital. They also presuppose that *all* development will be auto oriented, regardless of whether the actual residents, patrons, or employ-ees arrive by car, privileging sprawl over traditional walkable patterns of development.

The ideal path for reform-minded cities is to follow the formula set out by economist and parking policy guru Donald Shoup: correctly price the on-street parking and let developers determine how much off-street parking, if any, is necessary for each development.[4] By applying dynamic prices to street parking, in which prices shift in response to demand, cities can ensure that there will always be a few spots available, thereby reducing the incentive to cruise for an unpriced space. As a side benefit, Shoup notes, this would open up a new source of revenue for communi-ties, funding local street improvements and street upgrades.

As far as off-street parking goes, developers—not planners—have both the right incentives and local knowledge needed to determine how much off-street parking is necessary. After all, if a developer builds too much parking, they waste money, while if they build too little, they may have trouble selling or leasing out the space. Eliminating minimum parking requirements merely gives developers the flexibility needed to adjust the amount of parking to local conditions, perhaps building more in subur-ban areas and less in more urban areas.

As more and more cities and towns are looking to clear a path for infill development, minimum parking requirements have often been the first zoning rules to go. In 2017, Buffalo became the first major US city to abolish parking requirements, quickly followed by Hartford.[5] Innumerable suburbs and small towns, along with big cities like San Francisco and Minneapolis, soon followed.[6] Where minimum parking requirements linger, they have often been substantially reduced. Over the past ten years, cities like San Diego and Cincinnati have substantially reduced these requirements, often outright eliminating them near transit and in central business districts. While there's still a long way to go in eliminating this element of zoning, important progress is being made.

ELIMINATE OR LOWER MINIMUM LOT SIZE
AND FLOOR AREA REGULATIONS

Another reform that is gaining traction is to lower or eliminate minimum floor area and lot size regulations.[7] Minimum floor area requirements prohibit the construction of an apartment or home below some specified square footage. These rules will vary by zoning district. For example, in Des Moines, a single-story house cannot be smaller than 1,300 to 1,700 square feet—depending on the design and location—regardless of what prospective residents may prefer.[8] While cities often set minimum floor area rules for apartments, a common variation of this rule is to limit the number of apartments that may be in a given building based on its floor area. In New York City, for example, this is referred to as the *dwelling unit factor*, which in more liberal districts requires 680 square feet of floor area per apartment.

Similarly, minimum lot size requirements stipulate the amount of land that must be set aside for each house. Returning to Des Moines, the minimum lot size for detached single-family homes hovers between 7,500 and 10,000 square feet. Many municipalities may also define a maximum number of units per acre, but the effect is the same, in that it requires that some minimum amount of land be consumed per house built. Both minimum floor area and lot size rules can range *much* higher than these examples might imply. In New York City, for example, the effective minimum size of an apartment in certain districts can be as high as 1,560 square feet, while in suburban New England, minimum lot sizes often run well over two acres.

It's important to note that these rules have no basis in health or safety requirements. Minimum unit sizes, as determined by the actual building code, are often far smaller than zoning's minimum floor area requirements. The purpose of these zoning rules is merely to force houses and the lots they sit on to be bigger than they might otherwise have been. This, in turn, raises housing costs, providing local policymakers with a subtle way of excluding less affluent residents by way of setting high minimums. The development pattern that results from these policies—a landscape of McMansions on Potemkin estates—is also the groundwork for American sprawl.

Unlike single-family zoning or minimum parking requirements, uptake on minimum floor area and lot size reform has been underwhelming. This is too bad, as reforming these two rules would likely have a profound impact on American development patterns: for cities and towns along the coasts, scrapping minimum floor area requirements would allow the market to meet the burgeoning demand for "microunits" and "tiny houses," which can be as small as 280 square feet. And in the suburbs of the Sun Belt and Mountain West, where the overwhelming majority of US housing growth is now happening, lowering minimum lot sizes would result in more housing, less segregation, and less sprawl as cities expand outward.

DECRIMINALIZE INHERENTLY AFFORDABLE HOUSING TYPOLOGIES

Beyond these "low-hanging fruit" reforms, there are several important zoning reforms that have yet to make the transition from policy paper to reality. Key among them is the need for cities to remove barriers to new housing construction at the bottom of the market. As discussed earlier in this book, single-room occupancies (SROs)—which allow a resident to lease a private bedroom with a shared bathroom and kitchen—historically served as an invaluable source of affordable housing at the bottom of the market.[9] Indeed, SROs kept millions of Americans off the street. Yet new SROs are nearly always banned by zoning. Policymakers could change that tomorrow.

In the same spirit, municipalities—particularly suburbs and rural areas—should end zoning discrimination against manufactured housing.[10] Once synonymous with "cheap," manufactured housing today is often just as good as site-built housing, both from an energy efficiency and a durability standpoint, yet at around a third of the cost. After the initial manufactured housing boom of the 1970s, many municipalities in warm-weather states like Florida quickly clamped down on manufactured housing by way of zoning, for no other reason than to exclude less affluent residents. As with bans on SROs, zoning bans on manufactured housing mainly serve to criminalize the bottom of the housing market, while giving exclusionary suburbs another tool to keep the less affluent out of their communities. Both rules should go.

Taming Local Control

Not every municipality will be so eager to liberalize zoning. Indeed, the cities and towns that have undertaken policies like ending single-family zoning or dropping minimum lot sizes have been the exception. In most municipalities, the politics underlying restrictive zoning—namely, homeowner resistance to change—is rock solid, particularly among the most restrictive municipalities. The reality is that it will take oversight from higher levels of government to get most US cities, suburbs, and towns to make any meaningful reforms to zoning.

Happily, there is precedent: each municipality's power to adopt and implement zoning is strictly defined by state zoning enabling legislation. Despite the popular perception that zoning is a purely local issue, state governments ultimately have the final say over how local governments may regulate growth. With this power comes the right of the state to intercede when municipalities are abusing that power. After all, when one municipality decides to block new housing development or exclude certain classes of people, it can have a detrimental impact on the region as a whole, to the extent that it shifts development elsewhere or raises costs across an entire region. It's not only appropriate for states to intercede in such cases—it's exactly why state oversight exists.

State preemption of zoning has so far focused on setting up guardrails around local powers, restricting or altogether abolishing those elements of zoning that are most prone to misuse by ill-meaning municipalities. The idea here is to simply take broken tools out of the local zoning toolbox. In 2019, for example, Oregon voted to end single-family zoning in any municipality with a population over ten thousand.[11] In most Oregon cities, duplexes are now allowed anywhere residential is allowed, while in Portland, fourplexes are allowed in all residential zones. Similar bills to end single-family zoning statewide have been subsequently introduced in states as diverse as Nebraska, Virginia, New York, and Washington.

Other states have taken the alternative approach to ending single-family zoning, adopting statewide ADU ordinances instead. Since 2017, for example, California has required that each municipality adopt an ADU ordinance, which would allow extra housing units in all residential zones.[12] In addition to this mandate, the bill maps out the basic permitting processes (no excessive public review) and design standards (no untenable requirements), which municipalities might otherwise have used to continue to discreetly block ADUs. This sparked an early ADU permitting boom in cities like Los Angeles, where ADU permits jumped from 80 in 2016 to 6,747 in 2019.[13]

To further clear a path for ADU construction, California again liberalized ADU rules in a series of bills in 2020.[14] These changes included increasing the minimum number of allowable ADUs on each residential lot to two, tightening the permitting review process to 60 days down from 120 days, and preempting many of the ways that local governments continued to use zoning to block ADUs, such as minimum parking requirements and owner-occupancy requirements. As a result, single-family zoning—an institution that made increasingly less sense in the context of a statewide housing shortage—is effectively dead in California.[15]

Beyond single-family zoning, a raft of preemption bills has come after various other misuses of local zoning powers over the past few years. In 2019, Arkansas passed a bill preempting the power of local government efforts to impose costly design and building materials standards by way of zoning, above and beyond state building codes.[16] This power had exclusively been used in the wealthiest suburbs in each state, with the result being much higher housing costs. The bill also instituted an additional prohibition against municipalities placing a minimum floor area on single-family houses. On the other end of the political spectrum, Vermont is considering a statewide maximum for the minimum lot sizes that a local government may impose—5,400 square feet—as a way to reduce the state's infamously onerous local minimum lot size rules.

The unique thing about zoning reform is that within each of the states profiled so far—already a diverse medley in its own right—preempting the most often abused zoning rules has enjoyed wide bipartisan support. Across Oregon and Oklahoma, California and Texas, Republicans and Democrats alike could each find a compelling narrative to tell about the need for zoning reform—the former emphasizing housing production and economic growth through deregulation, the latter appealing to the need to end exclusionary zoning and contain sprawl. This speaks to the political wisdom of undertaking reform at the state level: removed from the NIMBYism that normally dictates local politics, liberalizing zoning becomes a political no-brainer.

Is There a Role for the Federal Government?

What about the federal government, that branch of government *most* removed from NIMBY influence? As with state involvement, there's plenty of precedent for federal involvement in zoning; after all, the federal government did draft and aggressively promote model zoning legislation beginning in the 1920s. As the federal government played an increasingly large role in underwriting national housing markets and financing state and local government beginning in the 1930s, this nudge turned into a shove, such that by the 1970s, the federal government was both widely financing local zoning ordinances and conditioning essential federal grants on zoning adoption. All of this is to say, the federal government helped to get us into this mess—it stands to reason that it has some obligation to get us out.

Even if you're skeptical of getting the federal government involved again in zoning—if only to right past wrongs—the federal bureaucracy's hands are likely already tied. Since the 1968 passage of the Fair Housing Act, the federal government has had an obligation to "affirmatively further fair housing" (AFFH) by taking on housing segregation and discrimination at the local level. For decades, this provision was largely ignored. But in 2015, the Obama administration acknowledged this obligation and began drafting an AFFH rule that would require municipalities to inventory patterns of segregation and adopt reforms—zoning reforms key among them—that would address the issue. While the Trump administration ultimately scuttled AFFH after toying with a revised rule, this statutory obligation to eliminate regulations that drive up housing costs and perpetuate segregation isn't going away. Indeed, as of mid-2021, the newly elected Biden administration has already signaled its intention to revive AFFH.[17]

But what would federal involvement in zoning reform even look like? One popular idea for decades was to use the same types of nudges that led many of America's cities and towns to adopt zoning in the 1920s. By convening commissions and putting out detailed reports on the problems with zoning, the thinking went, municipalities would see the light and change their ways. Beginning in 1968 with the Douglas Commission, nearly every presidential administration over the past half century has convened a blue-ribbon committee or released a major report designed to promote zoning reform.[18] Past gestures at meeting AFFH obligations have been even *more* superficial: at one point, the Department of Housing and Urban Development notoriously allowed AFFH-offending municipalities to "make it right" with antiracism poster competitions. It should go without saying that none of this has meaningfully impacted the patterns of segregation that are still actively enforced by local zoning.

A more realistic path toward zoning reform must involve the kinds of carrots and sticks that the federal government used to scale up zoning in the first place. On the carrot end, one popular idea has been to give out competitive grants and offer technical assistance to local governments interested in liberalizing their zoning codes. And with the federal government underwriting a lot of local government spending, there are a lot of potential sticks. For example, there is now a consensus on the need to condition major grants like the Community Development Block Grant and Surface Transportation Block Grant—major sources of revenue for local community development programs and transportation infrastructure, respectively—on local governments adopting meaningful zoning reforms, such as those discussed previously.[19] A similar proposal has called on the Federal Transportation Administration to condition funds for new transit investments on zoning liberalization.[20] After all, why should the federal government pay for the construction of new transit in municipalities that will use zoning to block any and all transit-oriented development?

Restrictive zoning persists in large part because its political coalition at the local level—typically vocal minorities of incumbent property owners—is rock solid, particularly in the small, homogenous suburbs where the misuse of zoning has been most egregious. One way to resolve this issue is to shift at least some oversight powers to the state and federal levels, where policymakers and public servants can take a more holistic approach. Local reforms to liberalize zoning are great. But if we are going to meaningfully rein in zoning, we will need a blend of state preemption and federal incentives to fundamentally change the politics that shape local zoning.

Turning Japanese

If looking to the federal government on zoning might seem crazy, what could we possibly learn by looking abroad? As it happens, more than you might think. The US is hardly alone in adopting something resembling zoning. Yet as that last sentence might imply, most of what other countries call *zoning* is dramatically different from what we in the US call *zoning*. In some cases, these systems are slightly better; in some cases, slightly worse.[21] For example, in France, the zoning rules are slightly more liberal—with little in the way of use segregation—but there are strict rules on density and massing. Meanwhile, in the United Kingdom, zoning is much stricter, with no such thing as as-of-right permitting—every development is strictly discretionary—and detailed rules surrounding both uses and densities.

But if there is another "zoning" system we have a lot to learn from, it's the Japanese system.[22] In Japan, zoning is determined at the national level. There are 12 general districts, which may be mapped by local planning authorities. Compare that to the US, where zoning is almost exclusively written at the local level, with each local government coming up with its own boutique regime. I can't say I have *ever* encountered a local zoning code with only 12 zoning districts—on the contrary, most municipalities have many dozens of districts. New York City, all too typical even despite its size, has by my count at least 105 zoning districts.

At the outset, these process differences give Japanese zoning two key advantages over American zoning. For starters, Japanese zoning is simple and legible nationwide, thereby reducing barriers to development. A developer in Osaka can easily figure out what they can build in Tokyo and vice versa, a fact that wouldn't be true of even a Milwaukee developer looking to build across the lake in Grand Rapids. Better still, having 12 national zoning districts blocks misbehaving municipalities from developing boutique zoning districts implicitly designed to block certain types of development. To return to New York City, for example, many of those 105 districts are carefully designed to allow only one particular development pattern, with highly prescriptive use and density rules. Many of the newer low-density "contextual" zones were explicitly written to ban apartments while locking in the existing scale. No such malfeasance would be possible under Japanese zoning.

These process differences also help to explain why the substance of Japanese zoning regulation is so liberal. Take use segregation. Japanese zoning doesn't have anything resembling single-family zoning. In even the *most* restrictive Japanese residential zoning districts, apartments and single-family homes alike are allowed as-of-right, as are small corner stores and certain professional offices—that is to say, the casual use mixture that defined many US residential neighborhoods before the rise of zoning. Further, Japanese zoning is hierarchical, meaning that less disruptive uses (such as houses or small shops) are allowed in areas otherwise demarcated for more disruptive uses (such as regional shopping centers or office towers), meaning that the optimal degree of use mixture can emerge organically.[23] Only the most noxious industrial uses are fully segregated into separate districts.

The way Japan regulates density is likewise quite liberal. While there are floor area ratio (FAR) rules in Japanese zoning, the rules dictating envelope—or the form a building can take, such as setbacks, heights, and lot coverage—are much more liberal. Take height limits: in the US, height limits are often used to restrict all future buildings to the scale of whatever already exists. Like the US, Japan does have a handful of zoning districts where heights are capped at three stories, the standard for low-rise development. But in the more common medium- to high-density zoning districts, Japanese heights simply require that taller buildings step back at predetermined intervals, based on the width of the adjacent street, not unlike New York City's 1916 zoning ordinance. This way of regulating building height addresses the actual light and air impacts tall buildings may have, without arbitrarily restricting densities.

Great though the Japanese zoning system may be, I wouldn't suggest holding your breath on the US adopting a national zoning law. Yet there is still a lot we can learn from Japan, namely that a simpler, more liberal approach to zoning is not only possible but quite desirable—after all, the Japanese zoning system has kept cities like Tokyo remarkably affordable, despite a rapidly growing population.[24] At the same time, Japan's unique system calls into question an article of faith central to US zoning: local control. As we know from preceding chapters, unlimited local control is far more likely to generate local problems—unaffordability, stagnation, segregation, and sprawl—than it is to generate local solutions. While twelve national zoning districts are unlikely, why shouldn't states define the zones that local governments are allowed to map? If our goal were to make zoning "less bad," we would do well to look to the east.

For the same reasons that likely made you pick up this book, there has never been a more exciting time to think about zoning: now more than ever, reform is in the air. Once sacrosanct, single-family zoning is now on the defensive, and minimum parking requirements are clearly on the way out. At the state level, policymakers and elected officials are taking seriously the need to curtail the worst abuses of local zoning powers. And in a development that would have seemed absurd a mere five years ago, zoning reform even emerged as a major issue in the 2020 presidential election, despite a growing consensus on the desirability of having more federal incentives to liberalize zoning. We have it within our power to liberalize zoning in a way that eases the housing crunch, expands economic opportunity, reduces segregation, and tames sprawl like never before. The widespread adoption of a handful of zoning reforms would be transformative for millions of Americans. What are we waiting for?

CHAPTER 8

The Case for Abolishing Zoning

If the present groundswell of activism is any indication, more and more Americans are now comfortable with the idea of overhauling zoning. So why *not* merely reform it? Can't we liberalize local codes, set up a few state-level guardrails, institute some positive federal incentives, and call it a day? The trouble is that, without much deeper changes to the policies, institutions, and norms that shaped the zoning we have today, any system that allows municipalities to comprehensively dictate land use and densities will inevitably trend back toward the current mess. As long as we encourage Americans to think of their homes as an investment and allow every small suburb to incorporate and determine what can and can't be built, zoning will always serve to perpetuate housing scarcity, stagnation, segregation, and sprawl. We can't tinker our way out of this one; the longer-term objective must be zoning abolition.

But what about all the good that zoning tries to do? Set aside all its flaws for a moment: Who wants glue factories in residential neighborhoods? Certain land uses in certain places and at certain scales can have unwanted impacts on their neighbors. Who wants new housing built without the public services and infrastructure to match? Without some form of zoning, the argument goes, developers will have no reason to consider these impacts, and city planners won't be able to ensure adequate infrastructure and public services. Zoning is meant to help us escape from this chaos by setting clear parameters on what can and can't be built in advance and planning accordingly, heading off land-use conflicts and clearing a path for efficient growth patterns that leave us all better off.

In reality, zoning just isn't that great at ensuring land-use compatibility among neighbors, often ignoring meaningful incompatibilities. Where zoning *does* attempt to prevent traditional impacts among neighbors—like noise or traffic—it often does so in a discriminatory way, solving the problem by shifting the burden to the poor and politically weak. Yet zoning focuses the bulk of its energies on preventing impacts—such as coded claims about how certain residents may change the "community character"—which don't deserve regulatory deference, let alone active state enforcement.

Similar issues plague zoning's attempts at growth management. Zoning now works largely untethered from what we normally think of as city planning. Indeed, many cities with a zoning code don't have any comprehensive plan at all, while many more only halfheartedly incorporate zoning into this broader plan, if at all. Meanwhile, the supposed "stability" brought on with zoning has been largely undermined by the recent shift away from as-of-right zoning and toward discretionary permitting. With mechanisms like variances, special permits, rezonings, and planned unit developments emerging as the norm, whatever claims that could be made about the power of zoning to lend stability to communities go out the window.

The issue with zoning is not that planners are bad at their jobs. The issue is that zoning asks them to undertake an impossible job. How could anyone map out the optimal mixture, scale, and location of every conceivable land use in an entire city? Zoning assumes not only that planners can project out the needs for every single type of housing or commercial use but also the scale at which it should all be built, and where it should all be built—and not merely for one slice of reality, but across the lifespan of a zoning ordinance, which can often extend well over half a century. In every other sphere of public policy, the idea that this anachronistic style of top-down planning can achieve even passable outcomes has been thoroughly discredited. Why is zoning any different? For the sake of our cities and the people who live in them, it's time we fundamentally rethink how we regulate land in America.

Why Reform Isn't Enough

In light of the current political realities limiting the scope of debate, focusing on zoning reform makes sense. Until the metaphorical Overton window opens up—a shift this book aims to help along—it makes sense for activists and policymakers to focus their scarce resources on causes like reforming local codes or adopting thoughtful state preemptions. But merely reforming zoning *cannot* be the end goal. The forces that made zoning so awful in the first place won't magically go away even if we succeed in scrapping single-family zoning or lowering minimum lot sizes. As long as zoning is still on the table, the very forces that made zoning so harmful in the first place will always pull it back toward the dysfunctional status quo. The only way to sustainably escape this trap is to abolish zoning.

As we discussed back in chapter 3, a zoning system that systematically inflates housing costs—particularly in high-opportunity regions—persists in part because it ultimately benefits a minority of affluent homeowners who call the shots in local elections. Short of dramatic changes in how we tax and finance housing in this country, American zoning will always trend toward excessive limitations on housing, with painful downstream consequences for housing affordability and economic growth.[1] Extreme though it may seem to us today, zoning abolition is the least unlikely way of sustainably improving housing affordability.

Similarly deep-seated forces will undermine efforts to tame zoning's role in perpetuating segregation and sprawl short of outright abolition. Consider the issue of who sets zoning policy: local government. Partly as a result of zoning, local governance in the US is unbelievably fragmented. In the Los Angeles metropolitan area alone, there are well over 350 municipalities. In some cases, these municipalities are just neighborhoods with the power to adopt zoning, with literal gates at the municipal boundaries and metaphorical gates in the zoning code. Many of these municipalities exist purely to adopt zoning as a way to exclude certain less privileged groups and artificially keep densities low, hoarding lavishly funded public services for affluent residents.

A small slice of metropolitan Los Angeles's incorporated municipalities, each with its own power to zone. This extreme fragmentation will make piecemeal local zoning reform difficult if not impossible. (Ian Rose, Blueschisting)

The extreme fragmentation of local governance in the United States makes a simple city-by-city approach to zoning reform a nonstarter: there are simply too many municipalities in need of reform, and proponents of the zoning status quo—NIMBY homeowners—heavily dominate those municipalities where zoning is at its worst. Even with state preemption taking the most abused rules out of the local zoning toolbox and federal incentives nudging on behalf of reform, municipalities and neighborhoods committed to exclusion will always find ways to use zoning to block housing and shift most new development out onto either less affluent communities or the loosely zoned suburban fringe.[2]

As long as zoning exists in the United States, special interests will find ways to suppress housing construction, our most prosperous and productive places will be held back, affluent municipalities will find ways to lock out the marginalized, and growth will be forced into a sprawling pattern. To exclusively focus on tinkering with every local zoning ordinance or building out to state allocation plans may help to hold the line—an admirable and important cause—but in the long term, it's likely to be a losing battle. Lasting reforms will only take root when we address the heart of the problem: it's time to abolish zoning.

Steelmanning Zoning

"All right, hold up," you may be saying. "Can we *really* abolish zoning?" So far, this book has focused on explaining how zoning works and the costs it imposes on society. But doesn't zoning also address certain issues? Before explaining why and how we could safely abolish zoning, it's worth first making the "steelman" argument for zoning—that is to say, the best possible case that could be made in its favor. The two most compelling claims that can be made for zoning are that it does two things. First, zoning separates incompatible uses, preemptively setting aside specified districts for each use to minimize unwanted impacts. Second, zoning allows planners to ensure that future growth occurs in the right places and alongside needed improvements to infrastructure and public services, thereby ensuring a high quality of life for both current and future land users.

Let's unpack the issue of land-use compatibility first. Some land uses, like some people, just don't go well together. That's because some land uses can have unwanted impacts on certain types of neighbors. Economists call these unwanted costs *negative externalities*. Consider a classic case: a glue factory. A glue factory emits smells and smoke, which can be disruptive to neighbors. This is a cost that the glue factory may impose on neighbors regardless of where it goes. Without some kind of intervention, the factory operator has no reason to consider this cost, as it falls on others. To switch over to legal jargon, the glue factory is a "nuisance," and if the behavior of land uses like it goes unchecked, we are all worse off.

Now consider a subtler example: a beer garden. At first, a beer garden might not seem like a nuisance. Indeed, for many, it might rate as an amenity. In many places, a beer garden might not impose any costs on neighbors at all. A beer garden in a commercial or industrial neighborhood, or way out in the countryside, is unlikely to offend anyone. But what happens when we move this beer garden into a quiet residential neighborhood? Beer gardens can be quite loud, with patrons merrymaking, glasses clinking, and bands playing. By moving the beer garden to such a location, all that noise—particularly late at night—could seriously hinder the ability of neighbors to comfortably live their lives. As with the glue factory's smoke, the beer garden's noise is a cost imposed on neighbors, which the operator might not otherwise consider.

Of course, those aggrieved neighboring property owners could always take the offending glue factories and beer gardens to court. But why sit around and let conflicts arise in the first place? Cities are full of such potential conflicts and many of them could be solved with an ounce of foresight. The idea of zoning is that we can preemptively address these conflicts before they happen by keeping potentially incompatible uses in separate districts. We know that glue factories are going to make most nearby nonindustrial uses unworkable, so zoning segregates them into separate heavy industrial districts, ideally situated near needed infrastructure and downwind from more sensitive uses. We likewise know that beer gardens are going to make residential neighbors uncomfortable, so zoning corrals them into commercial districts along major thoroughfares. Rather than try to ban glue factories or force beer gardens to keep it down, zoning aims to create a space for all uses, while ensuring that no use will impose undue burdens on anyone else, leaving us all better off in the process.

Similarly, zoning gives planners the ability to manage growth in accordance with a long-term vision. In one sense, this argument for zoning works like the first argument: without sufficient infrastructure and public services in advance of new development, growth may often impose unwanted costs on neighbors. For example, a brand-new mall along a two-lane country road may cause unending traffic, making the road practically unusable for existing agricultural users. Or a brand-new apartment building in a neighborhood with overcrowded schools may exacerbate the problem, reducing education quality for existing students. Thus, even innocuous growth in the wrong place, without inflicting any traditional impacts such as smoke or noise, may still have harmful impacts on the community.

But this argument for zoning is broader than the first argument, to the extent that these problems will also lower the quality of life of the residents, patrons, and employees of these new developments as well. After all, these new land users will have to deal with the resulting issues—congested roads and overcrowded schools—just as much as the existing land users. As with separating incompatible uses, this is a problem that we can solve with an ounce of foresight. If planners can decide where growth is going to occur, what form it will take, and at what scale it will unfold, they can direct growth away from areas unsuitable for growth. At the same time, planners can ensure the adequate provision of infrastructure and public services in those places marked for future growth. Zoning is the regulatory mechanism that turns foresight into action, allowing planners to preemptively determine where growth will and will not occur.

For the early North American city planning movement, managing growth in this way was a major priority. When rapid population growth in cities in the United States began in the late nineteenth to early twentieth century, activists from a range of disciplines found consensus on the need for a more active government role in planning out urban expansion, of both the vertical and horizontal varieties. Open space and transportation planning—heirs of the earlier Garden City and City Beautiful movements—were causes célèbre at early national city planning conferences, which began to meet in 1909. Housing overcrowding was likewise widely recognized as a major issue. These early planning discussions occurred at a time when growth was often haphazard, with new development overwhelming urban areas with density or spreading out into the countryside where basic infrastructure—such as paved roads or sewer connections—would need to be built ex post facto by underresourced municipalities.

When zoning first came online in the mid-1910s, solving these complicated and seemingly unrelated planning challenges all at once was a key part of the pitch. And the argument remains compelling to this day: by allowing planners to sit down and determine where every given land use may be allowed and at what densities, they can effectively rationalize urban land use "in accordance with a well-considered plan," an aspirational condition set out in the Standard Zoning Enabling Act. In addition to dealing with the problem of incompatible uses, zoning allows planners to deal with a host of other social issues, such as reducing densities in overcrowded quarters, concentrating growth along underutilized roads and transit lines, and ensuring parks and school sites are mapped out in advance of new development. Without zoning, solving these various issues becomes ever so slightly more complicated, potentially resulting in poorly planned communities that lower the quality of life of residents.

By design, this section has generously left out some of the less savory objectives behind zoning outlined in chapter 1, such as the desire for inflated property values or racial and class exclusion. But we shouldn't dismiss these arguments for zoning so lightly. Cities are a complicated mess of potentially incompatible uses, a problem that can destroy the quality of life for urban residents if left unaddressed. Growth without a commensurate plan for all the needed infrastructure and public services can be a disaster, as anyone who has visited the sprawling capitals of the developing world can tell you. Viewed from the right angle, the idea of zoning—the idea that planners can and should sit down and rationalize the distribution of land uses and densities in an entire city—is intoxicating at first glance. Yet as the next section will argue, it was all a dream.

Meanwhile, Back in the Real World

This is a comforting story—comforting enough, at least, to provide cover for the continued survival of zoning, even in the face of all of its obvious costs. But back in the real world, zoning has largely failed in achieving even its stated purposes. On the land-use compatibility front, zoning is a poor substitute for directly regulating the externalities that upset people, missing subtle differences between land uses while leaving the borders of districts exposed and shifting the burden of unwanted uses onto the less affluent. At the same time, zoning in practice works completely untethered from broader planning objectives and acts at odds with broader changes in land-use needs, resulting in an increasingly chaotic and unpredictable system of discretionary permitting. As with the last section, let's unpack each of these issues in turn.

FUMBLING LAND-USE COMPATIBILITY

The first issue is that zoning just isn't that great at ensuring land-use compatibility. Baked into the idea of zoning is the assumption that these externalities can be indirectly addressed by categorizing and sorting land use. If we know what kinds of impacts every land use might have, the thinking goes, we can shuffle them into appropriate districts and solve the problem of unwanted impacts. But in practice, it's much more complicated than that—few uses are so obvious in their impacts as glue factories. Indeed, even members of the same land-use categories rarely behave the same way in terms of the impacts they may have on neighbors.

Take cell phone stores, a land use often allowed in neighborhood commercial districts: your typical AT&T store wouldn't have any measurable impacts beyond a marginal increase in traffic. But a MetroPCS store, infamous for its practice of blasting music out onto the street, may have profound impacts on neighbors. According to the zoning ordinance, these are identical uses, appropriate in all the same places. Poorly tailored land-use categories like this—focusing on the superficial fact that both types of stores sell phones while ignoring their dramatically different noise impacts—abound in zoning ordinances, producing a steady stream of neighborly disputes even in the most aggressively zoned cities.

Worse yet, zoning's emphasis on districts often leaves residents powerless against unwanted impacts when the use in question is allowed. If a zoning district permits a given use—no matter how obnoxious—aggrieved neighbors will have to appeal to non-zoning forms of regulation or legal action to have land-use disputes resolved, undermining the very point of zoning. Recall the beer garden example from the last section: in theory, zoning addresses the noise impacts that a beer garden may have on nearby residents by putting the former into a commercial district and the latter into a residential district. But what happens when districts bump up against one another, as they necessarily must?[3]

Where zoning does endeavor to effectively separate uses based on classic externality issues, it often does so in two ways, each with their costs. The first strategy is to adopt overly conservative rules on land use—that is to say, by doubling down on rigid use segregation, with ever finer subdistricts specifying and separating ever finer land-use subcategories. Consider the case of a corner grocery in a residential neighborhood. To some, a corner grocery may be a welcome neighbor, providing daily necessities within walking distance. To others, it may be a source of unwanted noise and traffic. One person's amenity is another person's negative externality. As a further complication, the intensity with which these views are held may vary. Preemptively collecting and weighing all of this information for even a single corner grocery would be impossible, let alone for every conceivable land use.[4]

Zoning responds to this epistemological hurdle by radically reducing the frame of the problem, folding corner groceries into the "commercial use" category, which might include far more disruptive uses, such as car washes or gas stations, and banning them from residential districts altogether. It does so not because this is the optimal way to regulate land but because, if we are set on regulating negative externalities by way of use (as zoning tries to do) and preemptively addressing all potential land-use conflicts before they ever emerge (as zoning tantalizingly offers), this is likely the best we can ever do. By necessity, zoning must collapse land uses into arbitrary categories based on how planners interpret their theoretical impacts and fall back on simplistic use segregation or outright bans, regardless of the nature of the local preferences or the alternative remediation strategies that may exist.

The second way that zoning "solves" land-use compatibility issues is by off-loading its costs onto the less privileged residents of a city. Unsavory practices of this variety abound in zoning. Historically, industrial and bothersome commercial uses—uses like strip clubs and sex shops—were largely mapped in and around low-income residential neighborhoods.

It remains zoning "best practice" that single-family residential districts should be "buffered" from bothersome industrial and commercial districts by multifamily residential districts. This reflects zoning's modus operandi of protecting single-family houses at all costs, but it makes no sense from a land-use compatibility perspective. While a handful of generally more affluent homeowners may be better off, it comes at the cost of many hundreds more less affluent residents suffering a lower quality of life.

Go take a look at any zoning map for yourself and you will find multifamily residential districts overwhelmingly mapped along major corridors or adjacent to commercial or industrial districts. In cities like New York and Los Angeles, new high-density multifamily residential zones continue to be mapped along noisome elevated train lines or arterial roads or

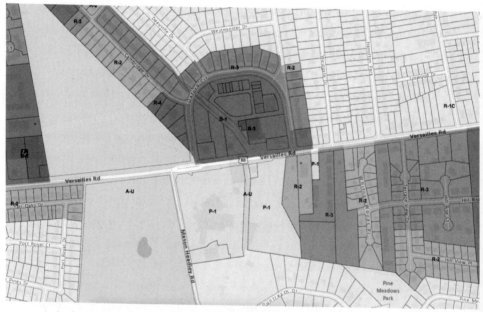

A clip from the zoning map of Lexington, Kentucky. Note how multifamily districts (which house more, but poorer, residents) are used as a buffer for nearby single-family districts (which house fewer, wealthier residents) from busy strip malls and commercial corridors. This is still considered zoning best practice. (Lexington-Fayette Urban County Government, Division of Planning)

adjacent to industrial zones with surprising frequency, while those areas best suited to residential living—such as quiet side streets or neighborhoods close to parks and schools—often remain off-limits to any development denser than a single-family house. Though this may make political sense, it can hardly be defended as a matter of efficiently and equitably allocating land uses and density.

While zoning codes often ignore what a normal person might think of as negative externalities—such as noise, smells, smoke, or traffic—they are often packed to the gills with regulations designed to address "externalities" that simply don't deserve regulatory deference. In many cases, the only externalities being regulated by zoning are the "costs" associated with strictly aesthetic changes to the neighborhood or people of different shades or classes entering the community. Take the appeal to "community character," a mainstay of zoning justifications. At best, this argument casts all change as imposing a kind of cost on neighbors, to the extent that it upsets some nebulous aesthetic quality of the neighborhood. In practice, this often means upholding yesteryear's ideal of a squat house on a vast lawn in the suburbs and arbitrarily capping building heights in cities, regardless of how much broader demographic and economic conditions have changed.

At worst, the "community character" appeal often serves as a dog whistle for preserving the existing racial and class makeup of a given place, particularly concerning zoning approvals that might allow less affluent residents to move into a neighborhood. The power to determine what gets built in any given municipality or neighborhood, after all, is the power to determine who gets to live and work there. Between the hand-wavy appeals to aesthetics and veiled exclusion, it should disturb zoning proponents that the "externalities" that zoning is most successful in addressing are those impacts least deserving of regulatory deference. Yet such is the sad reality of zoning's ambitious claims about rationalizing land-use patterns.

GROWTH MISMANAGEMENT

The second issue is that zoning hasn't been an effective growth management tool. At a procedural level, the relationship between zoning and planning is complicated: SZEA encourages municipalities to view zoning as a way to implement a broader comprehensive plan, which is supposed to track larger economic and demographic trends, lay out a general program for infrastructure, and set out a shared vision for the community. But in practice, a surprising number of municipalities enforce zoning without having any comprehensive plan at all. In New York City, for example, no broader vision or plan is guiding the current zoning ordinance, and New York City is hardly the exception.

Admittedly, the complete lack of a comprehensive plan is less and less common. Many states now require that municipalities engaged in zoning have *some* form of a comprehensive plan, which they must update every five to ten years. As a result, these documents are often thoughtful and up to date, incorporating extensive public input and useful data on emerging trends. The trouble is that few states require that zoning actually be consistent with these comprehensive plans, such that in most zoned cities, the zoning ordinance is both much older than the current comprehensive plan and at odds with both the values and socioeconomic realities identified therein. As a result, zoning, growth trends, infrastructure planning, and public service providers often work crosswise: municipal growth plans may call for new streets, transit lines, parks, and schools in one area, in response to population changes, while an anachronistic zoning plan may be forcing growth into a completely different area, if it allows growth at all. The unified plan for growth that early planners envisioned—with zoning in the driver's seat—just hasn't materialized.

As a result of this disconnect with broader planning processes, the substance of zoning is often totally out of sync with reality. Given how technically and politically challenging it can be to overhaul an entire zoning code, zoning codes often stick around decades after their dictates have stopped being relevant. As a result, many zoning codes are startlingly out of date. Take Austin's zoning code: written as it was in 1984, when the Texas capital was still a sleepy, midsized city, vast tracts of the city are reserved for low-rise, single-family housing and strip mall–style commercial. Fast-forward to the 2020s and Austin hosts the nation's fastest-growing tech sector and an explosive housing market, yet this zoning code survives, wasting land that might have been productively reused for office space or high-rise housing. Similarly out-of-date dictates can be found in nearly every zoning code—particularly for housing, where far less is allowed than is often needed—undermining the orderly growth and change of cities.

As a result of zoning predictably falling so out of sync with reality—to say nothing of planning objectives—the way we regulate land has become increasingly dependent on mechanisms that bypass the rules altogether, adding an element of lawlessness to the system.[5] In most major zoned cities, virtually every new development will now require some sort of variance or special permit, exempting any given project from this zoning mandate or relaxing that rule. Zoning maps, which rarely reflect the current demand for any given land use, must constantly be amended, such that the typical zoning map now looks like a Piet Mondrian painting overlaid on a street map. Zoning ordinances, meanwhile, have transformed from pamphlets into multi-binder affairs after decades of text amendments. Far from its original pitch as a system for providing certainty and order to cities, zoning is now largely illegible to the layperson and unpredictable in its application, undermining broader planning efforts to improve urban growth.

⸱⫶⫶⸱

While we should embrace opportunities for zoning reform as they arrive, we don't do ourselves any favors by limiting our scope to reform. If we want to build affordable, prosperous, integrated, and efficient cities, let's be forthright about it: zoning has failed at a basic level to achieve even its stated aims. It has failed as a way to ensure land-use compatibility, ignoring real externalities while focusing on frivolous concerns, and it has failed as a way to manage growth, frequently working in opposition to broader city planning goals and strategies. In the process of failing, it has left cities increasingly unaffordable, stagnant, segregated, and sprawling.

These failures flow not from any narrow problem with zoning as applied but with its very conceit: the idea that planners can—and should—tediously map out the appropriate land uses and level of density across an entire city every fifty years. Even if we could eliminate the bad incentives and special interests that will inevitably distort zoning, the real world is just too complicated for this ideal of planned efficiency.[6] The knowledge needed to rationally organize a city is subtle and context specific, as are the optimal remediation strategies. The demand for any given land use at any given location is subject to radical changes across time—even if a planner could ascertain it for one slice of time—beyond what any zoning ordinance could possibly be expected to plan for. As a result of this flawed underlying assumption, zoning—and the many bad predictions it has enshrined into law—has been a disaster, one that cannot be solved by minor reforms.

Yet at the same time, few would doubt that we need *some* ways of separating incompatible uses or tying growth to prudent planning. A city without mechanisms for keeping glue factories out of residential neighborhoods, or controlling nuisances like noise or traffic, or tying new growth to needed infrastructure and public service improvements, would be a disaster. Zoning hasn't been that mechanism—but that isn't where the conversation on American land-use regulation has to end. The good news, in a strange way, is that zoning is not only ineffective: it's also unnecessary.

CHAPTER 9

The Great
Unzoned City

Rising amid the rain-soaked coastal plains of Southeast Texas, Houston wouldn't seem real if it didn't in fact exist. Founded as a real estate venture in 1836, it became the capital of a brand-new republic before its first birthday—a title subsequently poached by Austin in 1839. Despite being nearly fifty miles inland from the Gulf of Mexico, it now has one of the nation's busiest ports, thanks in no small part to the near-total destruction of Galveston in 1900. Its sophisticated and growing space industry has largely been subsumed in the popular imagination by the apocryphal phrase "Houston, we have a problem." And when the city was slammed with some of the worst flooding in US history in 2017, it didn't lose population—on the contrary, it *gained* roughly thirty thousand new residents. Have I mentioned that it's the only major US city without zoning?

Houston is fascinating, not so much as a model city, but as a test case for non-zoning. And it basically works: unlike every other big city in America, the Bayou City makes no pretense at trying to comprehensively segregate land uses or control densities. There are no single-family zoning districts in Houston, no FAR regulations, no arbitrary distinctions made as to where shops can open up. This isn't a subtle fact about the city either: when the zoned American lands in Houston, they are liable to promptly be struck by parking lots reinventing themselves as apartment buildings with ground-floor retail, by entire neighborhoods of postwar subdivisions transforming into dense new townhouse districts, by old strip malls being reimagined as new satellite business districts. In the zoned city, any one of these developments would a major ordeal, the subject of endless permitting and raucous public hearings—in unzoned Houston, it just happens.

Far from the doomsday predictions made by the zoning pushers in bygone eras, unzoned Houston works just fine, thank you very much. Between 1970 and 2020, the city nearly doubled in population from 1.2 to 2.3 million, assuming the title of America's fourth-largest city. Attracting a blend of working- and middle-class Americans priced out of the rest of the country and international migrants seeking opportunity, Houston is now our nation's most diverse city, with dishes like smoked brisket banh mi and Cajun tacos to show for it.[1] Alongside this population boom, Houston now sports one of the fastest-growing metropolitan economies in the nation, with new industries like aerospace, health care, and advance manufacturing gradually weaning the city off its infamous dependence on oil.

There are many factors at play in the mind-boggling story of Houston, not the least of which include the happy invention of the air conditioner. Yet we shouldn't discount the importance of its unusually liberal approach to regulating land. Thanks in part to a lack of zoning, Houston builds housing at nearly three times the per capita rate of cities like New York City and San Jose.[2] It isn't all just sprawl either: in 2019, Houston built roughly the same number of apartments as Los Angeles, despite the latter being nearly twice as large. This ongoing supernova of housing construction—much of it infill development—has helped to keep Houston one of the most affordable big cities in the US, offering new arrivals modest rents and accessible home prices even amid seemingly endless demand.

But it isn't just about housing: non-zoning in Houston means not just an affordable home but an affordable home with access to the opportunities that only a global city can provide. Unlike in San Francisco or Boston, which hoard employment at Fortune 500 firms or enrollment in top universities among those affluent enough to cover the high price of zoning, Houston throws up no such barriers. To a degree witnessed in increasingly few American cities, almost anyone can just show up and build a new life in Houston. Once settled down, the prospective entrepreneur can pursue their dream without fear of antiquated use rules or onerous permitting hurdles, or the looming terror of obscene mortgage payments foreclosing the right to take a risk. The American Dream—a dream assaulted on so many fronts by zoning—is alive and well in Houston.

Houston is by no means a catchall model for planning. Like every other Sun Belt city, it struggles with segregation and sprawl—themes we turn to in the next chapter. Yet its continued success as one of America's most affordable and prosperous cities reveals the workability—indeed, the desirability—of non-zoning. But why didn't Houston adopt zoning in the first place? If it lacks zoning, why hasn't the city descended into chaos? And if not through zoning, how does the city regulate land? Houston is a profoundly weird place, resistant to seductive oversimplifications. But if we stare into the lone dissenter on zoning for long enough, we might start to develop a better sense for what comes after the arbitrary lines that have misshapen our cities—and how we might get there.

The Compromise That Saved Houston

So why *didn't* Houston adopt zoning like every other US city? The answer comes down partly to process. Unique among major cities, Houston subjected the adoption of zoning to a citywide vote. While most city councils had historically quietly adopted zoning after a few perfunctory public hearings, the Bayou City invited voters to decide on zoning in

An anti-zoning protest in Houston circa 1993. (Betty Tichich/©Houston Chronicle)

1948, 1962, and 1993. Voters rejected it each time—a reality that calls into question the often-postulated popularity of zoning.

The 1948 referendum was small, limited to roughly twenty thousand property owners.[3] Yet the results of the 1962 and 1993 referenda are much more telling, as each opened up the question of zoning to all. In both elections, zoning lost: 57 to 43 percent in the former and 52 to 47 percent in the latter. In both elections, the question of zoning quickly turned into a referendum on its inevitable use to raise housing costs and entrench segregation.[4] Naturally, opposition to zoning in both referenda came principally from working-class Houstonians of all races. In 1962, support for zoning tracked neatly onto a neighborhood's average annual income and rates of homeownership, with richer neighborhoods strongly in favor of zoning. In 1993, zoning likewise died on the shores of less affluent neighborhoods, where the low-slung apartments, corner stores, and shotgun houses that zoning so despises had already taken root.

While pro-zoning advocates in both referenda alleged the use of scare tactics by their opponents to dupe unsuspecting voters, the anti-zoning camp's concerns seem almost prophetic in retrospect. Zoning critics rightly dispensed with the comforting mythos surrounding zoning—that its purpose was to merely rationalize land use—and zeroed in on its tendency to restrict new housing construction, limit access to opportunity, institutionalize segregation, and force growth outward. Indeed, had Houston voters approved zoning in 1993, much of the city would now be constrained to a conventional R-1 district banning apartments and corner stores altogether.[5] Far from being duped, Houston's working-class residents exhibited a subtler understanding of the purposes of zoning than many contemporary planners and rejected it accordingly.

But the answer to why Houston remains unzoned also comes down to politics. Zoning proponents didn't merely lose the referendum—they were also tactfully bought off by being allowed to have something resembling zoning in their immediate vicinity. Indeed, the secret of non-zoning in Houston is that it depends on a system of emergent land-use regulations known as deed restrictions, which empower certain communities—principally middle- and upper-class homeowners—to effectively "opt out" of non-zoning, writing their own land-use rules for their own neighborhoods. In exchange, this compromise leaves would-be NIMBYs with little say over what happens in the rest of the city.

Deed restrictions are private, voluntary agreements among property owners—typically the homeowners of a particular subdivision or neighborhood—regulating how they can and cannot use their land.[6] These rules are literally tied to the deed, meaning that a property owner must agree to them as a condition of the sale. In most cases, deed restrictions regulate issues like land uses, building massings, architectural design, and maintenance expectations—that is to say, many of the provisions commonly found in a zoning ordinance. Since the failed 1962 zoning referendum, the city has enforced these agreements on behalf of the relevant parties, refusing to issue permits that run afoul of their provisions and bringing legal action against violators.[7] If a homeowner calls in to complain about their neighbor violating the deed restriction, a representative of the city will dutifully enforce its provisions on their behalf.

ARE DEED RESTRICTIONS BASICALLY ZONING?

Is this system of publicly enforced deed restrictions "basically zoning," as some might argue?[8] On the one hand, deed restrictions—like zoning—demarcate specified areas subject to a distinct set of stricter land-use rules. Both zoning and deed restrictions—in Houston, at least—are enforced by the government, principally with the aim of propping up home values and maintaining a certain quality of life. Some deed restrictions even enforce something resembling a beefed-up R-1 zone, with rules banning apartments and enforcing a strict two-and-a-half-story height limit, coupled with added provisions controlling the color of drapes or the frequency with which an owner must mow their lawn.

Yet the similarities end there. Where the rubber hits the road, Houston's system of deed restrictions is a significant improvement over zoning. For starters, deed restrictions only cover an estimated quarter of the city.[9] This is in stark contrast to zoning, which by definition applies citywide. Specifically, deed restrictions almost exclusively exist in those areas of the city with historical pockets of low-rise, detached, single-family housing. Industrial areas, commercial corridors, mixed-use and multifamily neighborhoods, urban vacant lots, and yet-to-be-developed greenfields are virtually never subject to their provisions. This means that roughly three-quarters of Houston—including its more dynamic sections, like Montrose and Midtown—are largely free to grow without anything even resembling zoning holding them back.

Another key difference between zoning and deed restriction is that the latter must be voluntarily opted in to. This serves to discipline deed restrictions in a way that is rarely true of zoning: if the rules are stricter than what prospective homebuyers might prefer, or not strict enough, or simply focus on the wrong concerns, this may translate into lower home values. This in turn nudges homeowners to think through the optimal form of land-use regulation to a degree that rarely happens with zoning. As a result, deed restrictions are rarely quite so strict as the most exclusionary zoning districts—there are thus few half-acre-plus minimum lot size districts in Houston. Likewise, the provisions of deed restrictions can vary in sync with the different land-use preferences that different communities may have.

Deed restrictions not only vary by preference across the city—they also evolve over time as those preferences change. Perhaps the biggest difference between zoning and deed restrictions is that deed restrictions usually go away once they have outlived their purpose. Unlike zoning, many deed restrictions come with a baked-in expiration date. After their initial term is up—usually twenty-five to forty years after adoption—deed restrictions depend on regular reapprovals, which take place at ten-year intervals. Historically, many deed restrictions simply expired after their initial term. While newer deed restrictions don't often disappear in this way, reapproval votes still offer an opportunity to periodically audit the rules. This can result in deed restrictions being incrementally liberalized—say, to allow accessory dwelling units in the face of rising rents, or home-based businesses in response to a global pandemic.

More commonly, unwanted deed restrictions will simply wither away by neglect. Unlike zoning, deed restrictions only survive to the extent that they are actively enforced—if certain rules are persistently ignored, or areas of the neighborhood are given a free pass, a court may eventually consider the deed restriction unenforceable. While Houston's system of public enforcement partly works to minimize this eventuality—if the enforcement costs are socialized, more enforcement will tend to occur—deed restrictions can and frequently do still lose the force of law as changing conditions make their provisions unworkable or undesirable. It might go without saying, but this is not an option for zoning, no matter how incoherent a particular zoning designation may become with time.

A CONTRARIAN CASE FOR DEED RESTRICTIONS

These deed restrictions, for better or worse, challenge Houston's reputation as a land-use free-for-all.[10] Yet they also run the risk of pulling the city into enforcing rules that reflect some of the less savory elements of zoning, inasmuch as they restrict housing supply, entrench economic segregation, and block densification. Why *should* the city publicly subsidize deed restriction enforcement? This brings us back to the political compromise underwriting non-zoning in Houston: by giving those homeowners with a strong preference for strict land-use regulations the rules they crave within their little fiefdoms, these groups stop agitating for a citywide zoning system that would do far more damage.

This is borne out in the history of Houston's zoning fights. The first serious push for zoning came not in 1948 but in 1939, three years after deed restrictions had expired in the large inner suburb of Montrose. The effort failed, but the pending expiration of deed restrictions in another neighborhood—River Oaks—formed the basis for the 1962 referendum. Not coincidentally, River Oaks was one of only two neighborhoods that supported zoning. It lost the referendum but won public enforcement of deed restrictions as a consolation prize in 1965, preventing further demands for zoning for a generation. Fast-forward to the mid-1990s, nearly thirty years after the major 1970s Houston building boom and right around the time that we would expect a new generation of deed restrictions to start expiring and—lo and behold—a third zoning referendum was held.

The history of zoning referenda in Houston tells a clear story: when their deed restrictions were threatened, middle- and upper-income homeowners started agitating for zoning. Public enforcement of deed restrictions should thus be understood as a clever compromise that ultimately keeps the broader city free of the dead hand of zoning: by granting those pro-zoning minorities the opportunity to voluntarily opt in to the restrictive land-use regulations they desire within their immediate vicinity, Houston is able to protect the vast majority of the city from the types of arbitrary use distinctions, density limits, and raucous public hearings that cause so much harm in every other US city. That is to say, in exchange for respecting pockets of private land-use regulation, Houston is able to grow, adapt, and evolve like no other city.

How Cities Organize Themselves

If deed restrictions control only around a quarter of the city, how does land use work in the rest of Houston? Hop in the car and let's take a drive around H-Town—everyone here drives, for better or worse. One of the first things you might be struck by is the extent to which Houston isn't pure chaos. Contrary to what pure zoning theory might lead you to believe, cities contain within themselves mechanisms for sorting out the most incompatible uses and making density make sense before zoning ever comes into the picture. Far from being an anarchic mess of factories next to homes and incoherent density patterns, the city exhibits much of the desired use segregation and density clustering that zoning is theoretically supposed to enforce. What gives?

As we're cruising along the 610 Loop—the thirty-eight-mile freeway that encircles Houston and broadly frames the urban sections of the city—you begin to notice that the industry that so terrified some early zoning proponents isn't exactly randomly distributed; on the contrary, it seems to be heavily clustered around key transportation hubs, like freeway interchanges, rail trunks, and those portions of the Buffalo Bayou east of downtown, which feed cargo out to the Gulf of Mexico by way of the Port of Houston. As we exit the freeway heading into town, you

begin to notice something similar with the more rambunctious commercial uses, like supermarkets or strip malls: they are almost exclusively
along the major corridors. It's almost as if someone is coordinating all of
this, and yet, you know Houston doesn't have zoning.

The issue of land planning can be reduced to one question: How do we
determine what should go where? While zoning tries to solve this problem through brute force, thinking through every conceivable land use
and where it should go, a more elegant solution reveals itself in Houston:
for the most part, the uses sort themselves out. Even before zoning, differ-
ing locational needs help to nudge the most incompatible uses apart:

- Industries need to be where land is cheap and transportation is
  accessible, and complaining neighbors are few and far between.
- Large office and commercial centers thrive on the visibility and
  access afforded by major corridors and transit interchanges.
- Residential developments are content to fill up the quiet side
  streets in between, along with inoffensive retail—think corner
  stores and cafes.

Homeowners don't want factories or malls showing up on their cul-
de-sacs—and they can rest assured that those factories and malls don't
want to open up on their cul-de-sac either. As the legal scholar Bernard
Siegan observed in his landmark study of Houston, the city achieves
much of what we might consider to be desirable use segregation while
allowing the harmless mixtures that make many pre-zoning neighborhoods so livable.[11]

Hop back in the car and let's cruise north along the South Freeway.[12]
We begin in Pearland, an outer exurb about thirty minutes from downtown, featuring detached single-family homes on spacious lots. As we
approach the 610 Loop, the Astrodome comes into sight, and behind
that, the Texas Medical Center—one of the largest job centers in the state.
The homes get incrementally smaller, as do the lots. We pass Museum

Park and start to hit congestion in Midtown, where dense new town-houses frame the foreground. Off in the distance, a shiny new light-rail car whizzes down a canyon formed by recently built apartment buildings, leading straight to the high rises of neighboring Downtown. For a city synonymous with non-planning, the density sure seems to follow certain patterns—indeed, it almost seems planned.

The same block of Midtown in 2010 and 2020. Thanks to Houston's lack of zoning, densities can rapidly increase in response to surging demand for urban living. (Google Maps)

The truth is, no one consciously designed these density patterns—as the former World Bank urban planner Alain Bertaud puts it, they represent an "order without design," a spatial order that emerges from the uncoordinated actions of many millions of people competing to occupy scarce urban land.[13] The key mechanism coordinating all of these individual plans is land prices, which signal the demand to occupy any given patch, relative to the supply of alternatives. If the price for land is high, it means that a lot of people—perhaps residents, perhaps business owners—want to occupy that space. To solve this problem and allow many people to occupy the same plot, developers effectively *create* more land by building up—substituting capital for land—which, in turn, raises densities.

The patterns of demand that drive density seem to follow a universal trend, from Toronto to Taipei: they peak at the center of a city and gradually fall moving outward. According to Bertaud, this comes down to the core function of cities as labor markets: employers want to be in central locations so they can tap into the largest labor pools possible, while residents want to be close to these hubs so they may maximize their choice in employment. Thus, densities peak at the historic central business district and gradually fall moving outward, with local peaks surrounding transit nodes. In Houston, a half dozen or so smaller satellite business districts—think Uptown, Greenway Plaza, or Texas Medical Center—puncture the gradient, but the effect is broadly the same.

We end our tour by pulling into an unassuming strip mall to enjoy some tamales, served piping hot with two cool Lone Star beers. None of this is to say that land markets resolve all possible conflicts, or that Houston has reached land-use planning nirvana. No city clears that bar—density quirks and land conflicts will always slip through, no matter how aggressively markets or zoning might militate against them. Yet as astute observers of urban life as far back as Jane Jacobs have observed, cities are host to spontaneous orders that—to a much greater degree than we might at first appreciate—lend cities a basic degree of organization.[14] And how could they not? Until one hundred years ago, this was how all cities worked.

Land-Use Regulation after Zoning

Houston may be free of zoning, but it is hardly free of rules—and not just of the amorphous variety imposed by land markets. As we discussed above, some of these rules emerge from the bottom up. Deed restrictions—the principal regulator of land use within the city's low-rise single-family residential neighborhoods—have sprouted up in pockets where demand for stricter land-use regulation is unusually high. In cases where no such deed restrictions apply, neighbors may often haggle their way to ad hoc agreements that help to avoid conflicts. As Siegan observes, it's not uncommon for homeowners' associations to simply pay off owners of abutting properties to avoid more offensive uses, such as gas stations or car dealerships.[15]

Houston is hardly without public land-use regulation either. Yet in Houston, unlike in the zoned city, these land-use regulations are overwhelmingly focused on actual nuisances, rather than hand-wavy concerns over community character. For example, Houston—like many cities—has a strictly enforced noise ordinance aimed at addressing a major quality of life concern otherwise ignored by zoning.[16] Land uses that generate added fire risk are strictly proscribed, as are activities that create unwanted smells.[17] Naturally, floodplain development—which risks worsening the floods that plague the city—is strictly regulated.[18] And a set of rules at the county level creates a framework for dealing with light pollution.

The city also proactively regulates specific troublesome uses. Where zoned cities attempt to identify and segregate every conceivable use—harmless or otherwise—land-use regulation in Houston reserves its attention for the particular uses that universally seems to bother people. Pursuant to city regulations, slaughterhouses—an early zoning boogey-man—must remain 3,000 feet from the nearest residence; oil wells cannot be within 400 feet.[19] Strip clubs and other adult-oriented businesses cannot be within 1,500 feet of a school or church; liquor stores and bars cannot be within 300 feet.[20] (Evidently, lust is more offensive than gluttony.) And the location of billboards is heavily proscribed throughout the city. Where markets fail, these types of rules fill the gaps, without all the added baggage of zoning.

Unfortunately, not all land-use regulation in the Bayou City is so wisely tailored. As legal scholar Michael Lewyn has pointed out, a handful of zoning-stye rules have seeped into the Houston Code of Ordinances over the years.[21] For example, the city imposes minimum parking requirements, which mandate the construction of off-street parking for various uses.[22] As a result of the Ashby high-rise incident—in which a developer attempted to build a twenty-one-story residential tower in the middle of an upscale single-family neighborhood—buildings over seventy-five feet must incorporate a thirty- to forty-foot buffer separating them from any nearby single-family home.[23] And hidden away in Houston's subdivision ordinance, one will find regulations covering setbacks and minimum lot sizes.

The good news is that these exceptions aren't nearly as dire as they may seem. Minimum parking requirements are clearly on the way out: in 2019 and 2020, Houston City Council exempted large portions of the city adjacent to downtown and along transit lines from such mandates. The city's recently adopted climate action plan goes one step further, calling for the complete abolition of minimum parking requirements by 2030.[24] And unfortunate though it may at first seem, the recently adopted residential buffering ordinance effectively squelched renewed chatter among pro-zoning forces, at minimal cost to the vibrancy of the city.[25] You can still build a seven-story tower in a non–deed restricted single-family neighborhood in Houston without much fuss, an almost unheard-of idea in zoned America.

The setback and minimum lot size rules, for their part, are likely no longer an issue. In 1998, Houston eased up on setbacks and dropped minimum lot sizes for single-family homes down from 5,000 to 1,400 square feet within the 610 Loop.[26] This effectively removed the final remaining barrier to widespread infill development in Houston—other than minimum parking requirements—allowing the thousands of post-war, ranch-style homes that had previously characterized the city to be subdivided into up to three new townhouses each. By one estimate, this change triggered the development of over twenty-five thousand new homes within the urban sections of Houston, dramatically densifying many of the city's neighborhoods and relieving pressure on housing prices amid surging population growth. In 2013, these reforms were scaled up to the city as a whole.

The reforms took a page out of the broader compromise that keeps Houston largely free of zoning: it gave opponents an "opt out" option.

A slice of Rice-Military, the Houston neighborhood being remade by the townhouse building boom. (Google Maps)

Blocks and neighborhoods with a strong preference against the liberal-izing reforms could—pursuant to 60 percent approval in a vote of all affected property owners—revert to lot size rules that broadly reflected existing conditions. On the one hand, this concession limited the scope of the reforms: some neighborhoods did opt out, nearly always revert-ing to the old five-thousand-square-foot minimum lot size. On the other hand, this minor concession allowed for one of the most dramatic reforms to land-use regulations among *any* US city in recent decades—a reform that has helped to make Houston more affordable, equitable, diverse, and sustainable.

How to Abolish Zoning in Two Easy Steps

What can we learn from Houston? The example of America's great unzoned city offers certain actionable insights as to how a would-be zon-ing abolitionist might prevent zoning where it does not already exist and incrementally unwind it where it does. Drawing on the lessons of Hous-ton, let's consider what an off-ramp for zoning might look like.

First, to stop the spread of zoning, the adoption of any new zoning code should be conditioned on supermajority support in an even-year public referendum.[27] Historically, zoning codes were adopted in a shady and undemocratic process, with city councils delegating drafting pow-ers to an appointed commission and summarily adopting its proposals, which were often heavily dictated by special interests. As the repeated failure of zoning referenda in Houston and various other cities in South-east Texas reveals, when residents are given an actual say on whether to adopt zoning, the process isn't nearly so seamless.[28]

Such requirements could always be adopted locally. In the aftermath of the 1993 Houston referendum, after repeated failures on the part of local elites to impose zoning on the city, a provision was added to the city charter forbidding the adoption of zoning absent majority approval in an election-year referendum. Few cities can be expected to tie their own hands in this way. To overcome this issue, and ensure that new zoning codes aren't slipped past local residents, a referendum requirement should be added to each state's zoning enabling legislation. States have it within their power to set the terms by which local governments administer zoning—conditioning its adoption on the supermajority support of the residents is a perfectly reasonable provision to add.

Second, state and federal policymakers should draw from the lessons of Houston in developing, promoting, and heavily incentivizing the adoption of a post-zoning system of land-use regulation that achieves the posited benefits of zoning, without its many manifest flaws. As we discussed above, Houston accomplishes this in two ways. First, by allowing those neighborhoods with an extreme preference for zoning-like regulations to voluntarily opt in to stricter rules—while leaving them with little say as to what happens outside their borders—and second, by narrowly and effectively regulating the specific uses and nuisances that actually upset people. More cities should adopt such provisions and—once fully operational—subject zoning to a public referendum.

What might this look like in practice? Imagine the town where many residents are unhappy with their zoning code and are wondering what comes next—a set of conditions that applies to many US cities. To tee up zoning abolition, local leaders should begin by addressing the major concerns locals may have with land use. First, the town should establish a mechanism whereby subdivisions and neighborhoods with preferences for tighter land-use regulations can develop and opt in to their own town-enforced deed restrictions after a supermajority vote among the affected property owners.[29] Second, the town should adopt rules putting safeguards around the location of universally disfavored uses—such as heavy industry—and clarify existing ordinances covering common nuisances like noise, lighting, and traffic. With rules addressing the most pressing land-use concerns in place, and the typical proponents of zoning allayed with an opt-out provision, zoning should be put to a citywide referendum and—if all goes according to plan—abolished.

The first of these reforms is unlikely to raise any eyebrows. Requiring a referendum is clearly within the state's powers, and few newly proposed zoning codes would be likely to clear such a hurdle. But at first blush, the second of these reforms might seem downright fanciful. Why would any local elected official undertake such a perilous course of reform? The skeptical reader should consider two crucial elements of the proposal. First, as briefly mentioned above, this post-zoning transition program should be heavily promoted and incentivized by state and federal grant-making authorities, not unlike the state and federal policy proposals discussed in chapter 7.[30] Municipalities that embark on a zoning abolition reform agenda should be rewarded, while municipalities that cling to a broken institution should feel the heat.

Second, this reform agenda is not merely theoretical but exactly how Houston has remained liberal and—as we discussed above with respect to minimum lot sizes—how it has further liberalized its land-use regulations. The ultimate lesson of land-use regulation in unzoned Houston is that, if a vocal minority of homeowners with unusually strong preferences for zoning are given what they want, they will leave the rest of the city alone. Once such groups are satiated with deed restrictions that perform roughly the same function—yet without doing all the damage of a typical zoning code—it's unclear that there will be any constituency for zoning left to raise a stink. And once zoning is out of the way, a lot of the other challenges facing cities become much easier to solve.

On August 25, 2017, Hurricane Harvey made landfall in Southeast Texas and proceeded to drop an estimated sixty-one inches of rain on Houston, smashing all previous rainfall records. The subsequent flooding killed eighty-eight people, damaged nearly a quarter of a million homes, and collectively cost an estimated $125 billion. In the immediate aftermath, national commentators scrambled to find a clean narrative to slot the disaster into, with many pointing to the potential for more such catastrophic events with the advance of climate change. Others opted to turn the carnage into a morality play, laying blame for the disaster at the feet of a conspicuous fact that Houston lacks zoning.

Needless to say, zoning had almost nothing to do with the flooding. Keeping grocery stores out of neighborhoods or lopping stories off the top of apartment buildings wouldn't have had any effect either way.[31] As Mayor Sylvester Turner rightly noted, "Zoning wouldn't have changed anything. We would have been a city with zoning that flooded." To the degree that the damage of Hurricane Harvey was a story of development run amok, this development was almost entirely in Houston's zoned suburbs, where regulators callously allowed development in floodplains and without sufficient stormwater infrastructure. Ironically, to the extent that Houston's lack of zoning made infill development easier, non-zoning likely *helped* to stem the tide of wetlands development and mitigate the damage.[32]

Houston is by no means a perfect city. In the same way that it reveals what non-zoning can accomplish when it comes to housing affordability or access to economic opportunity, it also exposes the need for non-zoning forms of planning in addressing issues of equity and sustainability. Other than wisely bypassing zoning, Houston planners until recently made nearly every twentieth-century planning mistake in the book, building out a city that—while laudably affordable and accessible—was in many respects inequitable and unsustainable.[33] Zoning is a *necessary* if not *sufficient* reform. Abolishing zoning doesn't mean the end of planning—on the contrary, it's only the beginning of a new chapter in planning.

CHAPTER 10
Planning after Zoning

There's a malaise haunting American planning. You feel it in the break-out rooms of planning conferences, in the halls of planning offices, in the classrooms of planning schools.[1] Attracted to the profession by high ideals, many planners have lost faith in the project of planning as it exists today. This is particularly true of the lowly land-use planner, a creature reduced to managing rezoning paperwork for an anachronistic zoning code and meekly taking notes as a motley crew of busybodies take turns shouting at them over a zoning variance.[2] The dreams that motivated planners, a once forward-looking profession that sought to remake the American cities for the betterment of all, now finds itself merely a reactive force, absorbed by the tedium of enforcing floor area ratios and demarcating use subcategories on behalf of unrepresentative interests.

Thus, the irony of planning under zoning: we relish in assigning pubs and delis and bakeries to separate use districts as we ignore the actual nuisances that bedevil urban life. We issue breathless press statements on behalf of equity, without a serious plan for promoting integration. We micromanage the setback of every building, as sprawl continues without the disciplining power of even a basic street plan. Zoning has utterly consumed planning, to the point that many city planning departments now do little that would resemble what a normal person might think of as planning. And it shows in the American landscape, an all too often inequitable and sprawling mess of disconnected cul-de-sacs, vacant strip malls, and inhospitable thoroughfares. Abolishing zoning doesn't mean the death of planning—on the contrary, it could mean the resuscitation of a once vibrant field.

What follows is a sketch of what planning might look like after zoning, a policy program for obtaining the supposed benefits of zoning—sorting incompatible neighbors and managing growth—without its many manifest costs. As we saw in the case of Houston, unexpected solutions will emerge—neighbors will develop novel systems of land-use regulations, and markets will broadly serve to sort out the most incompatible neighbors. Yet planning still has an important role to play. Land-use conflicts will always find a way to slip through, necessitating thoughtful rules for traditional nuisances like noise, vibrations, smells, and lights. Undoing the segregation entrenched by zoning will of course demand the active participation of planners. And we must revive planning institutions of yore, with planners thinking through plans for future streets, parks, and public facilities, in advance of growth and in a way that is fiscally and environmentally sustainable.

It's the Externalities, Stupid!

Back when I was a city planner in New York City, I received a call one morning from a resident of one of my community districts in Queens. The stressed voice on the other end of the line came from someone who hadn't had much sleep. The problem was a new neighbor, she said. In the ground-floor retail space next door to her second-story condo, a bakery had just moved in. There had always been shops and restaurants there, which she said she didn't mind, but this new bakery was different: they fired up their ovens at 4:00 a.m. to start baking for the day. This involved turning on an industrial fan, which woke her up and left her entire apartment shaking for hours. She raised these concerns with the bakery manager and his landlord but was quickly brushed off. What could city planning do?

After dutifully checking the zoning for her area, I explained that the bakery was a permitted use, so there likely wasn't anything city planning could do. The zoning was, at once predictably and inexplicably, silent on the issue of vibration, noise, or any of the other common impacts that drive conflicts among neighbors. A small bakery was allowed along any street with a C-1 zoning overlay, regardless of its impacts, so that was that. I didn't want to be the stereotypical "pass the buck" cog in a bureaucracy, so I talked her through the wording of noise and building inspection complaints she could make that might actually force an inspector to come out. I even explained that she could always speak to an attorney about her options. But, strange though it may seem, the way we regulate land use wasn't going to be of any help.

This call served not only as a reminder of the complicated spillovers that plague city life but of the extent to which our system of land-use regulation—zoning—totally fails to address them. But what does land-use planning look like after zoning? Rather than trying to address these spillovers by itemizing and segregating every conceivable use, planners should cut out the middleman and focus their attention on the specific spillover effects that bother people, supplementing the emergent forms of land-use regulation we discussed in the last chapter. The concept is simple: there are certain activities that planners know will impose costs on neighbors, from unwanted noise to trash-strewn lawns. For such foreseen impacts, more sophisticated regulation and enforcement may be the answer. And for the innumerable unforeseen conflicts that cities are constantly discovering, the solution may often be good old-fashioned mediation.

REGULATING ACTUAL NUISANCES

Take the issue of noise: if you live in a city, you likely don't need me to tell you that it is a key quality of life issue. Indeed, it's now well established that living next to a noisy neighbor or along a noisy street can be deleterious to mental and physical health: according to one 2018 survey of the literature, exposure to noise pollution increases sensitivity to stress, which in turn leads to higher blood pressure, resulting in a higher risk of heart attack and stroke.[3] One study conducted by the World Health Organization estimated that such effects have collectively meant the loss of 1.6 million healthy life years in Western Europe.[4] A separate study of the US found that taming noise could produce a collective benefit of $3.9 billion.[5] All this is to say that we know that noise is an issue, we broadly know how to measure and regulate it, and yet, planning seems weirdly uninterested in the issue.

It's easy to brush off noise—and innumerable issues like it, including light pollution, stormwater runoff, smoke and vibrations, untidy neighbors, and unwanted smells—as minor concerns. It's just a little noise, after all—what's the issue? Zoning certainly seems to take this position, silent as it is on the issue of noise. Yet these are the actual land-use issues that keep people up at night—in the case of noise, literally. City dwellers want some certainty about these types of nuisances, and planners should come up with a plan to give it to them. Regulating such impacts should be at the front and center of a reimagined post-zoning system of land-use planning.

While many cities have noise ordinances on the books—as well as ordinances for most other commonly acknowledged nuisances—these ordinances are often ambiguous, weakly enforced, and rarely coordinated with other land-use patterns. My hometown of Lexington, for example, prohibits various noise-generating activities, such as the use of leaf blowers or lawnmowers after 11:00 p.m.[6] But beyond the offenses listed, the city deploys few clear rules concerning permitted levels of noise. In New York City, as indicated earlier in this chapter, police and building inspectors with other priorities often halfheartedly enforce noise rules. And few American cities make any distinctions by geographic area, a peculiar oversight given that not all neighborhoods have identical noise preferences. Why should a sleepy residential street and a longstanding bar district be subject to the same rules on noise?

Unshackled from zoning, planners should rise to the occasion and take the challenge of mitigating these traditional nuisances seriously. Where ordinances regulating these baseline quality of life issues already exist, planners should dive into them, developing clear and measurable standards. New projects should be assessed against these standards, with regulations related to soundproofing or light design or impervious surface explicitly addressing the impacts that matter. These rules should be coordinated with existing land-use planning efforts and reflect actual conditions on the ground.[7] Perhaps most importantly, cities should work with city code enforcement officials to ensure robust and equitable enforcement. Clear rules tailored around specific nuisances, thoughtfully designed and consistently enforced, will go much further in advancing urban quality of life than zoning ever could.

PLANNERS AS MEDIATORS

Of course, not all unwanted impacts will fall into the mold of a traditional nuisance. In many cases, these impacts may not even be of the type that governments can or should regulate, such as architectural design—above and beyond basic health and safety—or the color of a building. As we saw in Houston, local communities are often quite sophisticated at organizing themselves and forming agreements like deed restrictions, which can establish emergent forms of land-use regulations, or haggling their way to mutually agreeable compromises. Planners should step in to help facilitate such arrangements, especially when historically marginalized communities are involved. Once we're outside the realm of traditional nuisances, rather than trying to a priori think through and solve every conceivable land-use conflict, planners should instead embrace their role as mediators, working with parties in conflict to find mutually agreeable resolutions.

It's not something they teach you in planning school, but in the day-to-day work of public sector planning, mediation is already a major part of the job. Indeed, give a planner a beer, and they're liable to share such war stories: One friend, a senior planner working in an unzoned context, once shared a story of a bar moving to town, sharing a property line with homes along the back of its lot. The bar was noisy and had lined the building's parapet with garish neon lights—both understandably offensive to nearby residents. After noise complaints fell on deaf ears, and their concerns about the light were altogether ignored, local residents turned to the planner and indicated their inclination to explore legal action.

Seeking to deescalate the situation and deal with the conflict, the planner made these concerns—and the risk of pending nuisance suit—clear to the bar owner, and after some mediation, the bar agreed to soundproof the building, remove the lights on the back of the building, and plant thick vegetation along the rear property line—small costs that avoided potentially costly and embarrassing litigation. Could prudent regulation or the narrowly averted nuisance suit have resolved these issues? Perhaps. But the benefit of mediation is that it solved the problem as it actually occurred, allowing parties to the dispute the ability to find the optimal resolution for that particular case.

As with code enforcement, mediation is already a service that some cities offer. Rather than ignoring such services, planners—newly free of dutifully administering the dictates of zoning—should play an active role, developing frameworks for equitably addressing recurring land-use conflicts, discovering and promoting emergent solutions, and advocating on behalf of communities traditionally victimized by such conflicts. If a revitalized land-use planning can get the balance of regulation and mediation right, the post-zoning city could end up being a far more pleasant place.

Desegregating the Post-Zoning City

According to the Othering & Belonging Institute at the University of California, Berkeley, over 80 percent of all large metropolitan areas in the US were more racially segregated in 2019 than they were in 1990.[8] Today, racial segregation is most acute not in the South but in the Midwest and mid-Atlantic regions. Black and Hispanic children growing up in such segregated neighborhoods continue to exhibit lower lifetime earnings, partly a function of continued disinvestment and poor public services. And economic segregation, or the segregation of Americans by income, remains equally pernicious.[9] This segregation is not an accident but the inevitable result of decades of interconnected policies, from housing finance to school districting, with zoning serving as the keystone.

Eliminating zoning is an important first step when it comes to rectifying this ongoing crisis. Without zoning, exclusionary suburbs and neighborhoods would lose their most effective mechanism for institutionalizing and maintaining both racial and economic segregation. Completely excluding more affordable housing typologies—such as smaller homes, townhouses, and apartments—would be much more difficult in a post-zoning world.

But abolishing zoning is just that: a first step, hardly sufficient to undo the damage that a century of state-enforced segregation has caused. In the same way that planners proactively segregated our cities, so they have an obligation to proactively advance integration.[10] In affluent neighborhoods and suburbs, this will mean integrating low- and moderate-income housing into high-opportunity areas—that is to say, those areas with easy access to good jobs and quality public services. In a gentrifying context, this will mean keeping low-income families in place as neighborhoods gradually desegregate. Let's consider each in turn.

OPENING UP THE HIGH-OPPORTUNITY AREAS

The first priority for planning in a post-zoning world should be opening up those affluent neighborhoods and suburbs that have historically used zoning to exclude the less affluent. Cities and states have at least two levers at their fingertips for determining where income-restricted housing goes. The first is the Low-Income Housing Tax Credit (LIHTC) program, a supply-side subsidy that facilitates the construction or rehabilitation of approximately one hundred thousand new income-restricted homes each year. While LIHTC is a federal program, state housing agencies are allocated a share of the tax credits and empowered to select which projects to subsidize. Historically, these projects have gone overwhelmingly in poorer, disproportionately non-White areas.[11] In fairness, many state housing agencies have recognized this issue and are working to right the ship. But states must double down on this momentum and prioritize projects that would allow more low-income Americans to find homes in high-opportunity areas.

The second lever is Section 8, otherwise known as the Housing Choice Voucher Program. As the name might imply, this is a demand-side subsidy, funded by the federal government and administered by local housing authorities, that provides vouchers to low-income tenants to help cover rent. The benefit of this arrangement is that it allows said households to choose where to live, with the market doing all the heavy lifting in terms of building and managing housing. As it exists today, Section 8 isn't fully funded—by one recent estimate, there are nearly three million households on the waitlist. Worse yet, certain provisions of the program serve to entrench segregation: Section 8 recipients in a city cannot take their voucher out to the suburbs, and voucher amounts are often too low to cover the cost of moving to a high-opportunity area. By fully fund-ing the Housing Choice Voucher Program, allowing vouchers to be used anywhere within a metropolitan area, and increasing voucher amounts for households seeking housing in high-opportunity areas, planners could help to ease patterns of segregation—and ensure that every American is housed doing so.

Prejudice against income-restricted housing is unlikely to go away any-time soon, and while abolishing zoning makes blocking that housing quite a bit harder, the most affluent suburbs and neighborhoods will always find ways to throw up barriers. How can states and cities over-come this challenge? One model to look to is Massachusetts's Chapter 40B program: in cities and towns where income-restricted housing makes up less than 10 percent of the housing stock, developers who propose projects wherein at least 20 percent of the units are income-restricted are entitled to permits.[12] In a post-zoning context, more states should follow a similar methodology, overriding local authorities when they refuse to accommodate their fair share of income-restricted housing. At the local level, municipal planners should follow a similar framework and use all available policy levers to ensure a fair distribution of income-restricted housing across neighborhoods, prioritizing its construction in high-opportunity areas.

LOCKING IN EQUITY

Gentrification is complicated. Over the past decades, middle- and upper-income households have surged back into cities en masse. With insuffi-cient housing construction in high-opportunity areas—largely a function of zoning—many have filed into historically low-income neighborhoods, from Bed-Stuy to Boyle Heights. On the one hand, this has helped to expedite the revitalization and desegregation of cities, even improving outcomes for those low-income residents who stay in place.[13] On the other hand, gentrification has raised understandable fears over the displacement of communities as rents and home prices rise. How can we enjoy the benefits of this type of neighborhood change, without all the costs? While removing the zoning barriers that block housing production in high-opportunity areas would go a long way toward easing the pace of change in low-income communities, it's clear that local planners need a plan.

One way to resolve this conflict is by leveraging all that new growth, incentivizing developers to incorporate low- and moderate-income units into new projects. Many cities do something like this today, either offering density bonuses in exchange for income-restricted units or simply outright mandating them. The former practice wouldn't be an option post-zoning—as arbitrary density restrictions would be gone—while the latter practice is simply counterproductive: as my colleague Emily Hamilton has shown, such inaptly named "inclusionary" zoning policies broadly serve to raise housing costs, without producing much new income-restricted housing.[14] Instead, cities should put their money where their mouth is, offering financial incentives—such as exemptions from impact fees, property tax relief, or expedited permitting—commensurate to the number of new income-restricted units that developers agree to include in new buildings. The additional tax revenue generated by new development in gentrifying neighborhoods could even fund these outlays.[15]

For a more systematic approach, planners should coordinate community land trusts. Under the community land trust (CLT) model, a nonprofit CLT purchases existing housing or develops housing on vacant, CLT-owned lots. The CLT then sells this housing at a discounted rate to a low- or moderate-income household, while retaining the land that it sits on in trust. As a condition of sale, this household agrees to sell the home at a price affordable to another low-income family, should they ever decide to move. In this way, CLTs create permanently affordable housing. Cities should endow CLTs with seed funds and give them preferential treatment for any city-owned land to be dispossessed. In gentrifying contexts, in particular, CLTs should play an active role in buying up what's called naturally occurring affordable housing—or housing that's affordable simply by nature of being old—and managing it subject to formal income restrictions.

When it comes to CLTs, Houston might once again serve as a useful model. According to the Dallas Federal Reserve, Houston is undergoing a wave of gentrification, with incomes surging in historically low-income neighborhoods near downtown.[16] In response, back in 2018, the Houston City Council granted the Houston Community Land Trust an initial endowment of $1 million with a goal of building or converting 1,100 trust homes within five years.[17] Working in conjunction with the Houston Land Bank—tasked with managing vacant, abandoned, and dilapidated properties—development is already under way: as of 2020, the Houston CLT has developed 21 homes at a median sale price of $75,000, well below the citywide median of $240,000. If they can pull it off, and eventually scale up the program, Houston might once again serve as a model for centering equity in a post-zoning city.

Reviving the Plan

If planners have an important role to play in supplementing emergent forms of land-use regulation and righting the wrongs of zoning, they have an absolutely central role to play in planning out the infrastructure and services needed to accommodate growth. By proactively planning out the public realm, planners can ensure that future growth is fiscally and environmentally sustainable, new public spaces and services—like parks and schools—are equitably distributed, and street networks adhere to patterns that enhance connectivity. In a post-zoning world, planners should take a realistic inventory of the development that's coming and develop workable infrastructure and services plans in advance of growth.

City planners should give up on trying to micromanage the dimensions of lots or the necessary off-street parking for barbershops and get back to what they do best: planning cities.

LET'S GET PHYSICAL

Why plan at all? Left without a plan, cities will have streets. But historically, these would typically end up a tangled mess of narrow leftover lanes at the edges of properties. While quaint for small towns or tourist destinations—who doesn't love wandering around the meandering streets of a medieval European town on vacation—these types of street networks are a disaster for mobility of all varieties, making it hard for large numbers of people to get into and out of central business districts every day. This type of unplanned growth likewise leaves little open space left for the public spaces that enrich urban life. The need for planning is especially poignant where sensitive natural settings—such as waterfronts or wetlands—are in play; without a plan in place before growth, such spaces will inevitably be gobbled up for private use, leaving everyone worse off.

Historically, planners took this charge seriously, carefully demarcating the public and private realms in advance of growth. In the sixth century BC, Hippodamus—a figure considered in the Western tradition to be the first city planner—planned out various Greek colonies, establishing a grid of streets with space set aside for an agora and an amphitheater. Early American planners followed in the mold of Hippodamus. In the late 1600s, surveyor Thomas Holme drew up Philadelphia's plan, a street grid stretching between the Schuylkill and Delaware Rivers, with a central plaza and four park squares. In 1811, New York City adopted its now famous grid plan for the island of Manhattan—Central Park came later, as development crept up the island.[18] Beyond ensuring easy mobility, access to parks, and sites for future public facilities, these plans created a framework for orderly growth, with plentiful space for underground infrastructure like utility lines and sewer pipes or new transit systems as populations increased.

Beginning around the mid-twentieth century, this type of nuts-and-bolts planning curiously fell out of fashion. As a result, many of the American cities that boomed after World War II are a mess of overbuilt arterials, underbuilt country roads, winding side streets, and dead-end cul-de-sacs, a public realm driven by the uncoordinated plans of developers, lacking any thoughtful planning oversight. The result is an urban form that is outright hostile to pedestrians and bicyclists, and barely functional for drivers. The siting of parks is irregular, if it happens at all, while school construction authorities must negotiate with developers for sites on the periphery as they scramble to accommodate population growth after the fact. It doesn't have to be this way: with a clearly defined public realm, planners could ensure that new growth is integrated into a broader vision, with new projects paying their way.

Map 5.1: 2040 Major Thoroughfare Map, City of Bastrop TMP

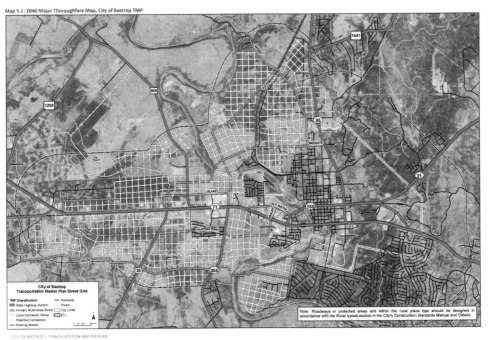

CITY OF BASTROP | TRANSPORTATION MASTER PLAN

The recently adopted Bastrop, Texas, street grid. Note how the proposed grid (white) contrasts with the existing street network to the southeast (black) that otherwise defines American sprawl. (City of Bastrop, Texas)

Happily, this type of physical planning has already started to make a comeback. Across the booming state of Texas, a handful of cities have embraced the grid in recent years. In 2019, the rapidly growing Austin exurb of Bastrop adopted a comprehensive plan that sketched out a street grid as growth expanded outward.[19] The plan had at least two big selling points: at once, it redirected growth away from flood-prone areas—a growing concern in recent years—and established a fiscally responsible plan for Bastrop. Unlike so much new development in American cities today, a new development in Bastrop will pay its way in property taxes, while ensuring that infrastructure and existing public services can be appropriately scaled up to accommodate new growth.

YOU GET WHAT YOU MEASURE

That said, it's not enough for planners to just draw lines on a map and call it a day. As the former World Bank planner Alain Bertaud has argued, planners must play an active day-to-day role in identifying, monitoring, and intervening on behalf of key quality of life indicators as growth unfolds.[20] What is the ratio of median home prices to median incomes? What share of the population has a commute over thirty minutes long? How far away is the typical resident from a park or a plaza? What is the daily average air quality index? As with traditional nuisances, these are the factors that can make or break urban life. Planners should shed their preoccupation with faddish and imprecise goals like "livability" and retool around metrics that can provide them real-time feedback about whether present planning and policy initiatives are working.

Undertaking this type of active planning means collecting and analyzing data on demographic, economic, and environmental trends on an ongoing basis: Where is new housing construction occurring? What types of people are moving into this housing? Where is new office development occurring? How do these people commute to work? How are temperature and precipitation patterns changing? What areas are newly threatened by extreme climate events? These are important questions that must inform every realm of public policy—from transit schedules to school construction to infrastructure upgrades to environmental protections—with answers that are evolving in real time. The days of planners writing a comprehensive plan and putting it on a shelf to gather dust are over.

At present, much of this forecasting and tracking work is done in a disorganized way—where it is done at all—with each agency coming to its own separate conclusions. And policy adjustments or new investments, more often than not, are in response to crises so bad that they can no longer be ignored, rather than any advanced reading of trends. This is no way to run a city. As a result of our inability to plan for and accommodate growth, new development often ends up imposing new burdens on neighbors. Cities need planners now more than ever. With a little foresight—dare I say, planning—we could do better.

ıı▮ıı

After a century of pretending like we have all the answers, perhaps an ounce of humility is in order. What will planning look like after zoning? I'm not entirely sure. And that's okay. We can be confident that it will involve a greater focus on nuisances, with baseline rules and context-sensitive mediation ironing out the conflicts that come with humans living in proximity to one another. Planners no doubt have some obligation to right past wrongs with the tools they have at hand, limited though they may be in this work by broader social forces. And our post-zoning future hardly means the end of city planning: the need for careful physical plans hasn't changed in the past thousand years, but our ability to thoughtfully manage cities has certainly improved.

The ideal system of planning urban land will doubtless vary by city. And why shouldn't it? Why should the same system of land-use regulation apply to flood-prone New Orleans and arid Phoenix, to shrinking Detroit and booming Dallas, to pre-car Boston and post-car Atlanta? After a century of zoning sucking all of the air out of the room, a lot of city planning experimentation is in order—who knows what new forms of land-use regulation remain to be discovered? Any uncertainty about what comes next shouldn't scare cities into inaction—on the contrary, it should serve as a welcome invitation to build a better system, as an intellectual adventure for the next generation of planners.

Conclusion

In 2016, the very first zoning code—a zoning code predicated on keeping poor Jewish factory workers away from the posh Fifth Avenue shopping district—turned one hundred. In 2026, the Supreme Court decision that deemed zoning constitutional—a decision that infamously referred to apartments as "parasites" and tacitly endorsed class segregation—will turn one hundred. These dual centennials may be interpreted in either of two ways. On the one hand, they might speak to the inevitability of zoning. Perhaps zoning has been chiseled too deeply into the American city to be removed, leaving wounds too deep to be healed. Maybe the best we can do would be to make zoning ever so slightly less bad. If that's the case, so be it.

On the other hand, the fact that zoning is only now turning one hundred might speak to the fact that we shouldn't take it for granted. A hundredth anniversary is as good a time as any for a reevaluation: when zoning first started to come online in the 1920s, nationwide alcohol prohibition was the law of the land, the doctrine of "separate but equal" defined race relations, and eugenics captured the imagination of governing elites. Needless to say, the times have changed. This is certainly true of cities: around the time of zoning's widespread adoption, nearly every major American city had doubled in size over the preceding thirty years, urban industry was still viable, and mass suburbanization and car ownership were only beginning to ramp up. The conditions that defined American cities have changed dramatically over the past century. Why shouldn't the way we plan them also change?

The premise behind zoning was simple: by defining and segregating different land uses and controlling densities, city planners would be able to separate incompatible neighbors and plan for orderly growth. Of course, it hasn't worked out that way; zoning has failed to efficiently deal with the messy spillover effects that nip at urban life, at once ignoring those activities that actually drive conflict—be it noise, or traffic, or lighting—while segregating uses with no such compatibility issues—such as the common zoning prohibition on small apartment buildings in single-family neighborhoods. At the same time, zoning has undermined the goals of efficient growth management, driving growth out onto the periphery, where new infrastructure must be built and new services must be provided, and out of existing urban areas, which could have accommodated additional growth at little additional cost.

Beyond merely failing to achieve its stated goals, the arbitrary lines that zoning imposes on our built landscape have deformed the American city. In cities like New York and Los Angeles, zoning has blocked new housing construction, perpetuating a housing shortage that has shoved millions of people into precarious financial situations, unsustainable commutes, and, in extreme cases, homelessness. In cities like Boston and San Francisco, zoning has locked American workers out of those places where they could contribute the most to our country, leaving us all poorer as a result. In cities like Milwaukee and Birmingham, zoning has institutionalized patterns of racial and class segregation and discrimination, preserving one of our nation's ugliest inheritances. And in cities like Nashville and Dallas, zoning has effectively mandated a sprawling, auto-oriented pattern of growth that is slowly chipping away at the health of our environment.

The good news, at this ominous centennial, is that it doesn't have to be this way. In the near term, reforming zoning makes sense. Reining in the worst excesses of zoning, such as single-family zoning, minimum lot sizes, and off-street parking requirements, would certainly help to stop the bleeding. But we can do better. In no uncertain terms, zoning should be abolished. Zoning is not only ineffective in achieving its stated goals— it's also unnecessary. In our focus on drawing district boundaries or listing out permitted uses, we have lost touch with the innumerable ways that cities organize themselves, from the natural use separation helped along by land markets to the bottom-up agreements formed by neighbors. Where these institutions fail, a robust set of impact regulations for new development and a civil service committed to managing—rather than stalling—growth would do a far better job than zoning at keeping neighbors happy and quality of life up. Now is the time to rediscover these lost traditions and start planning for what comes after zoning.

This isn't to say that an urban utopia lies on the other side of zoning. Housing will always be slightly more expensive in superstar cities. There will always be considerations besides the cost of living that keep folks from moving to thriving cities. Healing the scars of racism and classism will take decades, if not centuries. And national action—better yet, international action—is needed to address issues like climate change. Indeed, zoning isn't even the only policy that stands in the way of better cities. In some states, misguided environmental review mandates are at least as likely as zoning to stymie new housing. State-based occupational licensing regimes often keep people locked in place. Historic preservation tools are increasingly misappropriated toward exclusionary ends. And subdivision regulations play no small role in driving sprawl, mandating wide roads and wasted open space.

Yet the fact remains that abolishing zoning is a *necessary*—if not *sufficient*—change if we want to build a more affordable, prosperous, equitable, and sustainable American city. While earlier generations may have been excused for ignoring the arbitrary lines that have impoverished American life, we don't have that luxury. We now know beyond a shadow of a doubt that our century-long experiment with zoning has been a failure. But rather than a condemnation, this realization should serve as an invitation: an invitation to rethink the rules that will shape American life—where we may live, where we may work, who we may encounter, how we may travel—across the century to come. If the task before us seems daunting, the good news is that we have nowhere to go but up.

What Zoning Isn't

Back when I would tell people I was a city planner and that my job mostly involved working with zoning, I would get questions about everything from parks to schools to traffic. (Assuming they didn't just politely change the topic of conversation.) This is the kind of "city planning" that people can see in their everyday lives. If "zoning" is what most city planners do all day, surely it has something to do with stuff like designing public spaces and planning out new streets, right? The disappointing reality is that zoning has very little to do with these conventional planning objectives.

Even among those who understand that planning and zoning are different, it's common for people to misinterpret zoning as a catchall for controlling what does and doesn't get built. With respect to uses and densities, this is half true. But beyond that, the role of zoning is far more limited. For starters, zoning can only *stop* development; to start it, you need demand for new buildings and a stable of developers capable of profitably supplying it. Even before government regulation comes into the picture, a lot of use segregation and density patterns are as much a function of market demands and private agreements as they are of regulation.

But even among land-use regulations, zoning is hardly the only game in town. A host of federal, state, and local regulations having nothing to do with zoning—from wetlands protections to coastal plans to building codes—aim to ensure that most growth is safe and sustainable. Zoning is merely one tool in the planning toolbox.

At the risk of beating a dead horse, these distinctions are important to make if we are going to build a case for moving beyond zoning. Who in their right mind would support abolishing zoning if it meant allowing developers to demolish truly historic buildings or put smokestacks next to schools? Once you realize that zoning has little to do with these issues (as in the case of historic preservation) or that these issues are better dealt with by other forms of existing regulation (as in the case of emissions standards and school siting), the basis for its abolition will look a little less preposterous.

Zoning Isn't the Market

In 2019, Minneapolis became the first city to officially end single-family zoning, which banned apartments in approximately 70 percent of the city.[1] Adopted in response to a mounting housing shortage, the move quickly drew national attention as an unprecedented way to incrementally add more housing through duplexes and triplexes, where previously only single-family houses had been permitted.[2] But the coverage often seemed confused about how zoning works. More than a few articles, both favorable and critical, mused about how Minneapolis planners "banned" single-family zoning, with the implication being that single-family houses were no longer allowed. Elsewhere, opponents claimed that the zoning change would mean the imminent demolition of entire neighborhoods.

Both ideas suggest simple yet common mistakes about what zoning can and cannot do. Minneapolis didn't ban anything with this reform; rather, it *ended* a ban, namely on duplexes and triplexes in areas previously restricted to single-family housing. It certainly didn't ban single-family houses, which can still legally be built in every residential zone in the city. To the extent that this reform allows for some houses to be redeveloped or subdivided, it will be misleading to say that zoning *caused* this change. Rather, a booming demand for more homes, including units that are smaller and more affordable, is what will cause this redevelopment activity, if it happens at all; all planners did in this case was get an out-of-date zoning restriction out of the way.

Zoning alone cannot build a building; it can only ever *stop* something from being built. The overwhelming majority of buildings in the United States emerge from the complex market forces of supply and demand, not planning fiat. Apartments get built not because a zoning district allows them but because there are enough households seeking homes in a certain area, such that it pencils for a developer to assemble the capital, labor, materials, and land needed to build them. The same goes for every other land use, from residential subdivisions to strip malls to office towers to warehouses. The most that zoning can ever do is stop something that developers were otherwise going to build. If a project doesn't pencil, either through the rents it collects or public subsidies, it isn't getting built, regardless of the zoning.

For an example of this confusion manifesting itself in policy, take New York City. Vast swaths of the city's waterfront remain zoned for manufacturing as a kind of half-baked industrial policy, in the hopes that manufacturers will someday come back and build labor-intensive factories. Needless to say, this is unlikely to happen in our lifetimes. As a result, most of these sites simply sit underutilized, except to the extent that developers can find and exploit loopholes allowing them to build in-demand uses like self-storage facilities and budget hotels.[3] Zoning can try to block everything other than manufacturing, but it can't force any manufacturing to actually be built.

Indeed, before we even get to conventional land-use regulation, markets have their own ways of organically sorting uses and shaping densities. At a basic level, different types of uses will have different locational needs, allowing them to outbid other land uses for certain lots: retail will tend to congregate on busy corridors and street corners, offices will cluster around the central business district, and industry will locate out where land is cheap and transportation is accessible. Based on the preferences of residents, housing will mix in with the retail and offices and fill in the quiet blocks in between.[4]

The same is true of the way that markets rationally organize densities. Without going too deep into the weeds, density is principally a function of land prices, not zoning. A high land price means that a lot of people—be they residents or businesses—all want to be in the same place. To resolve this apparent conflict, developers substitute capital for land, building up rather than out, allowing densities to rise in high-demand areas. This density gradient is observed in cities around the world, as former World Bank principal planner Alain Bertaud observes, with densities declining as you move away from the busiest jobs clusters.[5] In this way, the market has a way of rationalizing uses and densities before explicit regulating mechanisms even come into the picture.

Zoning Isn't the Only Kind of Land-Use Regulation

Zoning is merely one form of regulation in a vast ecosystem of ordinances that control how buildings can be built. The most famous of these ordinances are building codes, which set basic standards for new construction. In the United States, these are mostly modeled after the International Building Code.[6] Unlike zoning, building codes are tailored around protecting basic health and safety, with special attention paid to structural integrity, fire abatement, and other specifications. Increasingly, building codes also regulate energy efficiency, prescribing certain materials and building methods as a way of minimizing energy consumption. A proposed building may be fully compliant with the relevant building codes while still being illegal under zoning.[7]

Another common ordinance regulating the development of land is the subdivision ordinance. At a high level, these ordinances regulate the breaking up of large lots into smaller lots. To use a common example, if you want to turn a large farm into a residential subdivision, the subdivision ordinance will supply the rules. Subdivision ordinances address two big issues. First, they record the newly created lots to a public ledger, ensuring that each new lot is compliant with dimension specifications and has a clear title. Second, they dictate what infrastructure must be provided in conjunction with a subdivision and to what specifications. These rules set the standard for elements like street design, wet infrastructure, and the required open space. Particularly with residential development

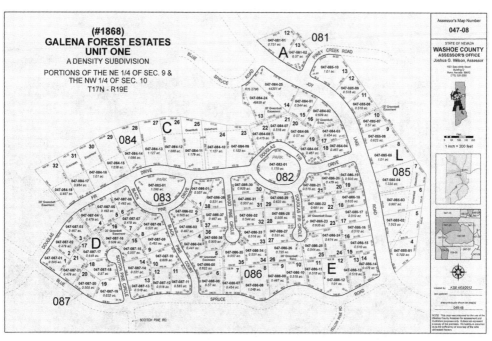

An example of a subdivision plat from Reno, Nevada. Note the focus on parcels, right-of-way design, and parks—that is to say, the key elements of physical planning. (Washoe County, Nevada Assessor's Office)

on the periphery, subdivision ordinances can often be far more conse-quential in guiding the growth of cities than zoning.[8]

While subdivision ordinances are mostly concerned with regulating development at the periphery, a small but growing number of cities apply design review to projects within already built-out neighborhoods. Design review attempts to strictly regulate the aesthetic considerations of a proj-ect, such as architectural style. Design review can vary a lot by city: In some cities, it may only apply to specific neighborhoods with distinct design characteristics; in others, it may apply citywide. In some cities, design review may be advisory; in others, it may be a necessary for secur-ing building permits. In some cities, acceptable design may be set out by a set of guidelines; in others, it may be an unpredictable, case-by-case process. The goal of design review is usually aesthetic uniformity, above and beyond the regimented massing standards imposed by zoning.

A photo of New York's Pennsylvania Station taken in 1910. The building was eventually demolished in 1968, prompting a surge in interest in the preservation of historic buildings. (Library of Congress Prints and Photographs Division)

But land-use regulation isn't just about what gets built. Since at least the 1960s, cities have grown just as concerned with what does and doesn't get demolished, by way of historic preservation. These ordinances commonly establish a commission to designate historic or landmarked properties and issue decisions on requests to modify said properties. Starting out, this work mostly focused on protecting high-profile landmarks, including Grand Central Station in New York City, motivating the 1978 case in which the Supreme Court sided with the preservationists.[9] Increasingly, these ordinances have been used to lock large swaths of cities in amber. In Washington, DC, for example, one in five buildings is now subject to some form of preservation restriction.[10] Like building codes, subdivision ordinances, and design review, historic preservation works independently of zoning.

Zoning Isn't Environmental Regulation

The overwhelming majority of environmental regulation in the United States flows from the federal government. The Clean Air Act deals with emissions, the Endangered Species Act aims to protect certain habitats, the Superfund program deals with contaminated land, and so on and so forth. Each of these laws, and many more like them, guide development and restrict land use in ways you might not expect. Beyond protecting rivers and streams, for example, the Clean Water Act also heavily regulates the development of wetlands. These laws often work in close conjunction with state governments. The Coastal Zone Management Act, for example, authorizes states to develop special land-use regulations for coastal areas. Other environmental regulations, such as those associated with stormwater and air quality management, are administered by state governments.

Beyond merely enforcing federal legislation, many states have adopted their own suite of environmental regulations. In a handful of states, such as Minnesota, larger projects may be required to conduct an extensive environmental review, which requires developers to catalog and mitigate any potential impacts. In states like California, nearly all development projects, whether public or private, are required to complete an environmental review.[11] NIMBY (Not In My Backyard) groups can—and often do—litigate on the basis of these reviews to scuttle projects. If you know of a local project that is tied up in the courts, more often than not, it's technically an environmental review issue rather than a zoning issue.[12]

Beginning in the 1960s, in what scholars call the "Quiet Revolution" in land-use regulation, states began establishing statewide and regional commissions that would review all local land-use decisions, typically with certain regional or environmental objectives in mind.[13] As with state-mandated environmental review, these reviews take into consideration environmental issues rarely considered by zoning. For better or worse, this provides an added layer of review that can slow down approvals and open projects up to a "double veto," requiring developers to successfully navigate multiple layers of regulatory oversight.[14]

All of this isn't to say that zoning never responds to environmental issues. In some states—though certainly not all—zoning ordinances are occasionally used as a tool of convenience for certain required environmental regulations. A minority of coastal states, for example, let local zoning codes set regulations like minimum setbacks from the coast. But environmental regulations like this are hardly intrinsic to zoning; most states set these standards statewide or require local governments to pass separate ordinances altogether for issues like farmland preservation or floodplain development. In Portland, Oregon, this is done through a state-mandated urban growth boundary; in Houston, this is done through a separate floodplain ordinance.[15]

Indeed, when you hear about plans to use zoning to address environmental issues, what's often happening is that policymakers are actually *scrapping* existing zoning rules that undermine environmental objectives.

In the case of New York City's Zoning for Coastal Flood Resiliency initiative, the key reforms included easing height and floor area rules that made flood-proof development illegal or prohibitively difficult to build.[16] Zoning itself simply isn't designed to protect the natural environment. Worse yet, as discussed in chapter 6, zoning is actively antagonistic to most environmental objectives.

Zoning Isn't City Planning

As discussed above, the most common confusion about zoning is that it's synonymous with city planning. This couldn't be further from the truth. While most people know, for example, that markets drive what does and doesn't get built, or that other kinds of regulations exist, few realize that zoning has little to do with things like streets, parks, or schools. Zoning is merely one tool in the planning toolbox, in theory subservient to broader plans, which should ultimately set the terms for growth. While the practice may vary a lot from city to city—and will often stray from planning theory—this section sets out the basic contours of how city planning works in the United States.

While we often speak of "city planning" as a discrete task, most cities have a veritable medley of plans in effect, most of which have nothing to do with zoning. In terms of regulating how a city will expand outward over time, a capital improvement plan, often abbreviated as CIP, can be far more consequential in shaping urban growth than any land-use regulations. The task of the CIP is to identify and budget all major capital improvements within the next five to ten years. These plans typically include major investments such as roads and bridges, sewer and stormwater infrastructure, and even new parks and schools.

To understand how this piece of paper—or more commonly today, PDF file—turns into urban form, consider how capital investments work in conjunction with market demand. Imagine that a city proposes to dramatically expand and straighten a winding, congested farm road connecting a far-flung exurb to the central business district, dropping the average commute along this corridor from sixty to thirty minutes. All else being equal, this will likely increase demand for housing out in the exurb, resulting in a low-density, auto-oriented development pattern.

On the flip side, imagine that a city proposes to close a lane of traffic along a major corridor to accommodate an overburdened bus line, turning it into a full-service bus rapid transit system, increasing frequencies and halving bus commutes all along the corridor. All else being equal, this will likely raise demand for housing close to the stations, resulting in nodes of townhouses and apartments along the corridor. You can imagine how other high-profile capital investments—such as a brand-new library or an upgraded park—would similarly drive urban form independent of zoning.

Other plans address other planning issues. In close conjunction with the CIP, most cities will also have a transportation plan, which focuses on minimizing congestion and improving mobility. Cities and suburbs alike will also usually have an open space plan, which maps out strategies for protecting and acquiring future open space. This is sometimes further broken out into a natural resource protection plan and a parks and recreation plan. In larger cities, it's common to have economic development and redevelopment plans, which may call for certain targeted investments. Similarly, a housing plan will track housing market trends and identify opportunities to preserve and build income-restricted housing. In large, spread out, diverse cities like Los Angeles and Houston, many neighborhoods will develop local plans for future growth.[17]

In theory, all of these plans, along with zoning and various other forms of land-use regulation, are meant to be coordinated by a comprehensive plan. This is *the* essential planning document, setting out the vision for a community across a "planning horizon," which usually spans twenty to thirty years. While a comprehensive plan lacks the legal force of any given ordinance—such as a floodplain or subdivision ordinance—the plan's legal force comes from the assumption that it will guide all other local plans, ordinances, and public investments.

Historically, the comprehensive plan was a dry document, passed after a single public hearing by the local planning commission. Today, planning staff will typically undertake drafting only after conducting extensive public outreach that, in most major cities, includes regular meetings with key stakeholders, dozens of focus groups and design charrettes, and various surveys to uncover a shared vision for the future of the city. The final document will usually also pull together data on the key demographic, economic, and environmental trends that will guide future growth, a high-level planning history, and an inventory of local assets. Happily for the lay reader, comprehensive plans are also increasingly readable and well illustrated—go browse through your local comprehensive plan if you haven't already.[18]

The relationship between zoning and comprehensive planning can be confusing. As originally intended by the framers of modern American planning, zoning is meant to be developed in compliance with a broader comprehensive plan, which usually includes a future land-use map.[19] The expectation is that planners should be informed by extensive public outreach, research into demographic and economic trends, and an awareness of challenges and opportunities before sitting down to write zoning.

The reality can vary quite a bit by state. In some states, such as Minnesota, a comprehensive plan is required before local governments can undertake zoning, with strict guidance on how the plan must be written. Indeed, Minnesota state law stipulates a consistency requirement, which requires that zoning remain fully compliant with the vision set out in the comprehensive plan. Most states are less strict. In many, such as Ohio, comprehensive plans are encouraged but not required for zoning. A surprising number of cities, such as New York City, undertake zoning without any comprehensive plan at all. But where they exist, as they do in most cities, the comprehensive plan—not zoning—is widely recognized as the bedrock of local planning.

ı ı ı ı

Unlike the market, zoning doesn't build buildings—it can only stop them from being built. Other ordinances cover common issues like subdivisions, design, and historic preservation. Federal and state regulators are in the driver's seat on protecting the environment. And within the broader universe of city planning, zoning is largely secondary to the various other planning mechanisms that guide urban growth. As we discussed in chapter 2, zoning is about segregating land uses and capping densities. That's it.

Abolishing zoning would still leave all the planning institutions that most people know and like—such as parks planning and traffic management—in place. Even without zoning, planners will still sketch out streets, protect historic buildings, and control the development of wetlands. At the same time, abolishing zoning would also leave certain dysfunctional planning policies—such as excessive preservation, or NIMBY environmental lawsuits—in place. As seen in part III, zoning abolition must be appreciated as a *necessary*, if not *sufficient*, change for building more affordable, prosperous, equitable, and sustainable cities.

Of course, this isn't to say that zoning is inconsequential. On the contrary, as part II argues, despite its seemingly limited scope, zoning *has* had a destructive effect on cities, which is why we should abolish it.

Acknowledgments

Like any work worthy of your time, this book is the result of many minds—I simply have the honor of putting my name on the cover.

In late 2019, I sent Tyler Cowen a grant proposal setting out my plan to spend 2020 cranking out blog posts and writing research papers. Since I knew he was interested in moonshot ideas, I tacked on one or two lines about a peculiar little book critiquing an obscure area of policy. Within forty-eight hours, I was on the phone with Tyler sketching out the contours of the book you now hold in your hands. In no uncertain terms, *Arbitrary Lines* would not exist without his early encouragement and the generous support of the Emergent Ventures fund.

Nor would it exist without the professional home provided by the Mercatus Center at George Mason University. In February 2020, I packed up my bags and moved from New York City to Washington, DC, to start a six-month fellowship with the Urbanity division. I was reluctant to move, but, as good urbanists, Salim Furth and Emily Hamilton gently reminded me of benefits of proximity. (One month later, we would all be working remotely!) In addition to being dear friends and colleagues,

Salim and Emily—along with Kevin Erdmann, Jamil Khan, and Tracy Miller—provided constant intellectual enrichment and invaluable early feedback.

Of course, anyone can put together a manuscript. It takes an editor to turn it into a book. For that, I am endlessly grateful to Heather Boyer and the team at Island Press. Her probing questions and thoughtful feedback helped to transform this book from a wonky treatise into something that a normal person might actually like to read. (To the extent that it remains the former, I take all the blame!) Shane Phillips kindly introduced us. Earlier on in the process, Garrett Brown decoded the dark arts of book publishing, providing extensive mentorship during the challenging early days of drafting and pitching the book proposal.

Last, but by no means least: Austin Woods came up with the title, a slight improvement over the working title of *Against Zoning*. (Evan Tindle and Adam Carrico made a good faith effort at coming up with alternative titles.) Weekly pandemic-era conversations with the Bertauds and the Ikedas enriched my thinking on cities throughout drafting. Michael Manville and Paavo Monkkonen found me a new home at the University of California, Los Angeles. Sylvia Valiente kindly hosted me in the home stretch of manuscript revisions. And Katarina Hall has been my companion through it all, a rock amid a maelstrom of a year.

I hope everyone mentioned above—and innumerable others who have supported me along the way—will take some pride in anything that is insightful, interesting, or important in this book. I take sole responsibility for everything else.

Notes

INTRODUCTION

1. Molly Boesel, "Home Prices Reached Highest Annual Growth Since 1979," CoreLogic, August 3, 2021, https://www.corelogic.com/intelligence/home-prices-reached-highest-annual-growth-since-1979/.

2. Erick Trickey, "How Minneapolis Freed Itself from the Stranglehold of Single-Family Homes," *Politico*, July 11, 2019, https://www.politico.com/magazine/story/2019/07/11/housing-crisis-single-family-homes-policy-227265/; Todd Gill, "Fayetteville Eliminates Minimum Parking Requirements," *Fayetteville (AR) Flyer*, October 7, 2015, https://www.fayettevilleflyer.com/2015/10/07/fayetteville-eliminates-minimum-parking-requirements/; Angie Schmitt, "Hartford Eliminates Parking Minimums Citywide," *Streetsblog*, December 13, 2017, https://usa.streetsblog.org/2017/12/13/hartford-eliminates-parking-minimums-citywide/.

3. Certain experienced planners may prefer to skip this section as needlessly restating what they already know; certain lay readers may prefer to skip it for its unavoidable wonkiness. Both should resist the urge, as this constitutes the less-exciting-yet-necessary vegetables of the book!

CHAPTER 1: WHERE ZONING COMES FROM

1. This historical norm can even still be found in American neighborhoods that were built out before the 1910s.

2. For an entertaining history of the City Beautiful movement's epoch, beginning with the World's Columbian Exposition in 1893, see Erik Larson, *The Devil in the White City: Murder, Magic, and Madness at the Fair That Changed America* (New York: Vintage, 2004).

3. For an excellent survey of the economics of skyscrapers, see Jason Barr, *Building the Skyline: The Birth and Growth of America's Skyscrapers* (Oxford: Oxford University Press, 2016).

4. For a history of the Great Migration, see Isabel Wilkerson, *The Warmth of Other Suns: The Epic Story of America's Great Migration* (New York: Vintage, 2011).

5. For a full history of the streetcar suburb phenomenon, see Sam Bass Warner, *Streetcar Suburbs: The Process of Growth in Boston, 1870–1900*, 2nd ed. (Cambridge, MA: Harvard University Press, 1978).

6. Sonia Hirt, *Zoned in the USA: The Origins and Implications of American Land-Use Regulation* (Ithaca, NY: Cornell University Press, 2014) refers to this tradition as "spatial individualism."

7. Histories of the American suburbs abound. Robert Fishman, *Bourgeois Utopias: The Rise and Fall of Suburbia* (New York: Basic Books, 1987) and Kenneth T. Jackson, *Crabgrass Frontier: The Suburbanization of the United States* (Oxford: Oxford University Press, 1987) are both well regarded.

8. Robert M. Fogelson, *Bourgeois Nightmares: Suburbia, 1870–1930* (New Haven, CT: Yale University Press, 2007) colorfully characterizes this period as one of "bourgeois nightmares."

9. For a full history of covenants and the pursuit of "permanence," see Fogelson, *Bourgeois Nightmares*.

10. As formulated by economist Bruce Yandle, "Bootleggers and Baptists: The Education of a Regulatory Economist," *Regulation*, May–June

1983, political reforms depend on coalitions among Baptists, who provide moral cover for the cause, and bootleggers, who have a financial stake in the cause.

11. M. Wolf, "The Prescience and Centrality of *Euclid v. Ambler*," in *Zoning and the American Dream: Promises Still to Keep*, edited by C. Haar and J. Kayden (Chicago: Planners Press, 1989), quoted in Hirt, *Zoned in the USA*.

12. For a complete history of the road to the 1916 ordinance, see Seymour I. Toll, *Zoned American* (New York: Grossman Publishers, 1969).

13. Robert H. Whitten, a key framer of New York City zoning, would go on to be one of the earliest zoning consultants, working on codes in Cleveland, Columbus, Dallas, Providence, and Atlanta. In many cases, these ordinances had overt racial segregation objectives, eventually forcing the Georgia Supreme Court to strike down Atlanta's ordinance. See Michael Allen Wolf, *The Zoning of America:* Euclid v. Ambler (Lawrence: University of Kansas Press, 2008), 29.

14. The original ordinance is quite short and worth reading for yourself. See City of New York Board of Estimate and Apportionment, "Building Zone Resolution," adopted July 25, 1916, https://www1.nyc.gov/assets/planning/download/pdf/about/city-planning-history/zr1916.pdf.

15. In the next chapter, we will dive deeper into how zoning works today.

16. As Wolf, *Zoning of America*, explains, American zoning was heavily shaped by the pursuit of constitutionality.

17. Jesse Barber, "Berkeley Zoning Has Served for Many Decades to Separate the Poor from the Right and Whites from People of Color," *Berkeleyside*, March 12, 2019, makes the developer connection, an underappreciated and perhaps unexpected constituency for early zoning, https://www.berkeleyside.org/2019/03/12/berkeley-zoning-has-served-for-many-decades-to-separate-the-poor-from-the-rich-and-whites-from-people-of-color.

18. Duncan McDuffie, "City Planning in Berkeley," *Berkeley City Bulletin*, March 15, 1916.

19. Notably, as of 2021, Berkeley is gearing up to be among the first cities to abolish single-family zoning. See Supriya Yelimeli, "Berkeley Votes for Historic Housing Change: An End to Single-Family Zoning," *Berkeleyside*, March 25, 2021, https://www.berkeleyside.org/2021/03/25/berkeley-single-family-zoning-city-council-general-plan-change.

20. As I understand, Hirt (*Zoned in the USA*, 165) first stitched this together, drawing on Mel Scott, *American City Planning Since 1890* (Berkeley: University of California Press, 1971).

21. Charles Henry Cheney, "The Necessity of a Zone Ordinance in Berkeley," *Berkeley City Bulletin*, March 18, 1915, 165.

22. Articulated by Berkeley City Attorney Frank V. Cornish in remarks given to the Berkeley City Club in 1915, quoted in Ben Barlett and Yelda Barlett, "Berkeley's Zoning Laws Wall Off Communities of Color, Seniors, Low-Income People and Others," *Berkeleyside*, June 13, 2017.

23. Hirt, *Zoned in the USA*, 165.

24. B. J. Bither, "A Factory Zone Necessary for Industrial Development in Berkeley," *Berkeley City Bulletin*, 1915. Note this is a kind of proto-fiscal zoning.

25. Today, virtually every zoning code deploys a "flat" approach to use segregation, foreclosing the possibility of *any* use mixing.

26. The first petition requested that single-family zoning be mapped in posh Elmwood Park as a way to block a proposed "negro dancehall" (Hirt, *Zoned in the USA*, 156).

27. Department of Commerce Advisory Committee on Zoning, "A Standard State Zoning Enabling Act," 1926.

28. While segregation didn't seem to be a principal motivation for Hoover, racial language colors his rhetoric in peculiar ways, characterizing single-family homes as "expressions of racial longing." Richard Rothstein, *The Color of Law: The Forgotten History of How Our Government Segregated America* (New York: Liveright, 2017), 61.

29. An in-depth history of the committee and its work can be found in Ruth Knack, Stuart Meck, and Israel Stollman, "The Real Story Behind the

Standard Planning and Zoning Acts of the 1920s," *Land Use Law* (February 1996).

30. Department of Commerce, "Standard State Zoning." As with the 1916 ordinances, the SZEA is short and surprisingly readable. Isn't old legislation wonderful?

31. Department of Commerce, "Standard State Zoning."

32. Robert McKenzie, *The Metropolitan Community* (New York: McGraw Hill, 1933), quoted in William Fischel, *Zoning Rules!: The Economics of Land Use Regulation* (Cambridge, MA: Lincoln Institute of Land Policy, 2015); Toll, *Zoned American*.

33. As quoted in Wolf, *Zoning of America*, 55.

34. This decision is why conventional US zoning, defined by its preoccupation with use segregation and strict density limits, is often referred to as *Euclidean zoning*.

35. As Rothstein (*Color of Law*) extensively documents, the overtly racist intentions of these conditions were often coupled with a condition that homes be subject to a racial covenant.

CHAPTER 2: HOW ZONING WORKS

1. As is the norm in planning practice, this book uses zoning *text*, *code*, and *ordinance* interchangeably to refer to this document.

2. Hence my heavy use, with apologies, of hedge words like *usually* and *typically* in describing how zoning works.

3. Lexington-Fayette Urban County Government Planning Office "Zoning Ordinance" (2021) offers a typical example, but check your local zoning code for another example, https://library.municode.com/ky/lexington-fayette_county/codes/zoning_ordinance.

4. More on this in the section "How Zoning Changes."

5. As we saw in the last chapter, this was a key element that differentiated zoning in New York City and Berkeley; the Berkeley model won out, resulting in the strict use segregation that characterizes US cities today.

6. For more on America's exceptional insistence on use segregation and privileging of single-family housing relative to other systems of land-use regulation, see Hirt, *Zoned in the USA*.

7. For example, R-1 will usually denote a low-density detached single-family residential zone, while R-2 might denote a slightly denser detached single-family, attached single-family, or duplex residential zone, depending on the municipality.

8. Alternatively, if your lot were assigned an FAR of 0.5, you could only build five thousand square feet of floor area on this ten-thousand-square-foot lot.

9. Research consistently finds that minimum lot size rules are among the most binding zoning regulations. For more on this, see M. Nolan Gray and Salim Furth, "Do Minimum-Lot-Size Regulations Limit Housing in Texas?" *Mercatus Research*, May 1, 2019, https://www.mercatus.org/publications/urban-economics/do-minimum-lot-size-regulations-limit-housing-supply-texas.

10. More on the role of building regulations in the appendix.

11. We will talk more about minimum parking requirements when we talk about the relationship between zoning and the environment. But for a deep dive into this topic, see Donald Shoup, *The High Cost of Free Parking*, 2nd ed. (New York: Routledge, 2011).

12. See City of Charlotte, North Carolina, "Code of Ordinances," Table 12.202 Minimum Required Off-Street Parking by Use.

13. Quoctrung Bui, Matt A. V. Chaban, and Jeremy White, "40 Percent of the Buildings in Manhattan Could Not Be Built Today," *New York Times*, March 20, 2016, using data compiled by Stephen Smith and Sandip Trivedi.

14. These boards vary widely in terms of professionalism and have often been criticized for the ad hoc nature of their operations. For more on this, see Jesse Dukeminier Jr. and Clyde L. Stapleton, "The Zoning Board of Adjustment: A Case Study in Misrule," *Kentucky Law Journal* (1962), https://core.ac.uk/download/pdf/232593299.pdf.

15. For an early study of this issue, see Dukeminier and Stapleton, "Zoning Board of Adjustment."

16. The esteemed professor who taught the planning law course in my master's program was less polite about the latter phenomenon, characterizing it as little more than legal extortion.

17. See Olivia Gonzalez and Nolan Gray, "Zoning for Opportunity: A Survey of Home-Based-Business Regulations," Center for Growth and Opportunity, March 11, 2020.

18. A fairly typical example, the zoning text for Lexington, Kentucky, tops out at 319 pages as of early 2020.

19. For more on form-based codes, see Form-Based Codes Institute, https://formbasedcodes.org/.

20. For more on performance zoning, see Lane Kendig, *Performance Zoning* (Chicago: Planners Press, 1980).

CHAPTER 3: PLANNING AN AFFORDABILITY CRISIS

1. This book does not aspire to be a literature review, but the curious can begin with "The Economic Implications of Housing," a survey of the literature by two pioneers in this space, Edward Glaeser and Joseph Gyourko.

2. The YIMBY moment is unique in that it's perhaps the first social movement to find its roots in the blogosphere. Adam Hengels would coin the term *market urbanism* in 2008. Later joined by Stephen Smith and Emily Hamilton, *Market Urbanism* would quickly establish itself as a major proto-YIMBY blog. In 2011, *New York YIMBY* began providing real estate news with a pro-development orientation. Matt Yglesias took the idea of easing up on zoning mainstream through outlets like *Slate*, and Kim Mai-Cutler would later pen the masterpiece of the YIMBY blogging genre, "How Burrowing Owls Lead to Vomiting Anarchists (Or SF's Housing Politics Explained)" for *TechCrunch* in 2014, providing succor for the early Bay Area YIMBY movement.

3. The Biden administration quickly followed, declaring its intent to tackle exclusionary zoning.

4. In *Barriers to Shared Growth: The Case of Land Use Regulation and Economic Rents* (2015), the Obama administration's Council of Economic Advisors set out a bold zoning reform agenda, while under the Trump administration, Secretary of Housing and Urban Development Ben Carson made zoning reform a priority.

5. See US Census Bureau, "Home Value and Homeownership Rates: Recession and Post-Recession Comparisons from 2007–2009 to 2010–2012," American Community Survey Briefs, November 2013, https://www2. census.gov/library/publications/2013/acs/acsbr12-20.pdf.

6. Chris Salviati, "2019 Cost Burden Report: Half of Renter Households Struggle with Affordability," Apartment List, October 9, 2019, https:// www.apartmentlist.com/research/cost-burden-2019.

7. Paul Centopani, "Home Prices Grow at the Fastest Annual Rate Since 1979," *National Mortgage News*, August 3, 2021, https://www.national mortgagenews.com/news/home-price-growth-rate-hits-42-year-high.

8. New York City Department of City Planning, "How Much Housing Is Built As-Of-Right?" March 2019.

9. Scholars have taken to calling this set of policies *exclusionary zoning*. As we observed in chapter 1, this exclusionary function was seen by zoning's framers as a feature, not a bug.

10. Emily Badger and Quoctrung Bui, "Cities Start to Question an American Ideal: A House With a Yard on Every Lot," *New York Times*, June 18, 2019, https://www.nytimes.com/interactive/2019/06/18/upshot/ cities-across-america-question-single-family-zoning.html.

11. Subdivided homes, which may host two or three modest apartments in a space that previously housed a single household, have historically served as a valuable source of affordable housing. When my paternal great-grandmother left rural Kentucky and moved to Louisville with her children—my grandmother and great-aunts—they lived in an apartment on the second floor of a divided-up old mansion in Old Louisville.

Today, this house has been reassembled and could not legally be subdivided a second time, owing to local zoning and historic preservation provisions.

12. While duplex zones are mapped with some regularity, apartment zones are often nonexistent in suburbs. And where apartment zones are mapped at all, they are often adjacent to industrial zones and other unpleasant uses, explicitly to use less affluent residents as a "buffer" to protect wealthier residents.

13. A setback forces a building to sit a certain distance back from a specified lot line. The floor area ratio is the ratio of building floor area to lot area, effectively a restriction on density. Lot coverage rules control how much of a lot must be left unbuilt.

14. City of Frankfort, Kentucky Code of Ordinances: Title XV: Chapter 152, Section 4.18. An earlier draft of this book used Lexington, KY's R-4 district as an example of a zoning district where strict massing standards made the theoretically allowed uses practically unworkable—happily, reforms in 2020 resolved these issues.

15. For an excellent study of SROs, which he refers to as residential hotels, see Paul Growth, *Living Downtown: The History of Residential Hotels in the United States* (Berkeley: University of California Press, 1994).

16. For more on the importance of SROs to groups at risk of homelessness, see Peter H. Rossi, *Down and Out in America: The Origins of Homelessness* (Chicago: University of Chicago Press, 1990).

17. While hardly glamorous, manufactured housing is often a substantial step up from the alternative, which in rural areas is often an informal shack. The Appalachian trailer that my mother grew up in was hardly luxury, but compared to the shacks that much of the Fletcher clan lived in, it was a clear improvement. President Lyndon Johnson would use one such Fletcher clan shack for a photo opportunity announcing the War on Poverty in 1964.

18. See Charles Haar, "Zoning for Minimum Standards: The Wayne Township Case," *Harvard Law Review* 66, no. 6 (April 1953).

19. Shoup, *High Cost of Free Parking*.
20. Lexington-Fayette Urban County Government Planning Office (2021), Sections 8-21, 8-33, and 8-39.
21. Assuming two standard 8'6" by 18'4" parking spaces and an adjacent 12' travel lane, the total space consumed is roughly 650 square feet. See Todd Litman, "Parking Requirement Impacts on Housing Affordability," Victoria Transport Policy Institute, January 20, 2009.
22. Shoup, *High Cost of Free Parking*, chap. 5.
23. Ironically, this "as-of-right" function was a key selling point used by early zoning framers to ensure buy-in from developers.
24. You can see why city planning departments are often treated as revenue-generating agencies for the purpose of public finance.
25. On top of the tens of thousands of dollars the applicant had to spend on a team of environmental consultants, any local opponent of the project with a couple hundred dollars to spare will also have standing to further delay the project with a frivolous lawsuit challenging the environmental review in court.
26. Combined with the risk of creditors or partners dropping out of the project, these delays can and often do kill projects.
27. As Katherine Levine Einstein, David M. Glick, and Maxwell Palmer, *Neighborhood Defenders: Participatory Politics and America's Housing Crisis* (Cambridge: Cambridge University Press, 2019) find, those who speak at public hearings in opposition to housing are often highly unrepresentative of their communities, both demographically and in their opposition to new housing. The authors find that speakers at public hearings are systematically more likely to be elderly male homeowners and to be far more opposed to housing than the average local resident.
28. Inflation, simply put, is the phenomenon whereby the same dollar buys fewer goods—i.e., it declines in value.
29. William A. Fischel, *The Homevoter Hypothesis* (Cambridge, MA: Harvard University Press, 2005).
30. By increasing the standard deduction and instituting a new mortgage cap of $750,000, the Tax Cuts and Jobs Act of 2017 substantially scaled back

use of the mortgage interest deduction and state and local tax credits. At time of drafting, Democratic members of Congress are currently trying to roll back some of these reforms. Capital gains treatment of home sales remains unusually generous.

31. As Joseph Gyourko, Jonathan Hartley, and Jacob Krimmel, "The Local Residential Land Use Regulatory Environment Across U.S. Housing Markets: Evidence from the New Wharton Index," NBER Working Paper Series (December 2019) note, the actual zoning on the books is often comparably strict in interior cities.

CHAPTER 4: THE WEALTH WE LOST

1. For a deep dive into the "geography of genius," see Eric Weiner, *The Geography of Genius: Lessons from the World's Most Creative Places* (New York: Simon and Schuster, 2016).

2. See Ryan Avent, *The Gated City* (self-pub., 2011).

3. Hannah Ritchie, "How Urban Is the World?" Our World in Data, September 27, 2018, https://ourworldindata.org/how-urban-is-the-world.

4. For a similar reason, Uber opted to open an AV research office in the Steel City—to be close to existing AV labs affiliated with Carnegie Mellon University.

5. Economists prefer to call these "thick" labor markets.

6. My father, for example, at one point specialized in designing the door handles of Toyota minivans. This degree of specialization—and the better door handles it produces—would not be possible without a truly massive labor market.

7. Alain Bertaud, *Order without Design: How Markets Shape Cities* (Cambridge, MA: MIT Press, 2018), chap. 2.

8. Recall from the appendix that land prices drive density in that high land prices incentivize the efficient use of land through increased density.

9. Enrico Moretti, *The New Geography of Jobs* (Boston: Mariner Books, 2013), 128.

10. While clusters may rebuild themselves in areas where housing is cheaper—be it tech in Austin and Denver or finance in Dallas and Charlotte—these clusters take decades to emerge, with a lot of potential productivity and innovation lost in the interim. Worse yet, what happens when these cities, which are all subject to zoning, run out of vacant land and become just as expensive as today's superstar cities?

11. Adam B. Jaffee, Manuel Trajtenberg, and Rebecca Henderson, "Geographic Localization of Knowledge Spillovers as Evinced by Patent Citations," *Quarterly Journal of Economics* 108, no. 3 (August 1993); Hyuk-Soo Kwon, Jihonh Lee, and Sokbae Lee, "Knowledge Spillovers and Patent Citations: Trends in Geographic Localization, 1976–2015," *Economics of Innovation and New Technology* (2020).

12. Edward Glaeser, *Triumph of the City: How Our Greatest Invention Makes Us Richer, Smarter, Greener, Healthier, and Happier* (London: Penguin Books, 2012), 29.

13. Luis M. A. Bettencourt, Jose Lobo, Dirk Helbing, Christien Kuhnert, and Geoffrey B. West, "Growth, Innovation, Scaling, and the Pace of Life in Cities," *Proceedings of the National Academy of Sciences of the United States of America* 104, no. 17 (April 2007), https://www.ncbi.nlm.nih.gov/pmc/articles/PMC1852329/.

14. Jane Jacobs, *The Economy of Cities* (New York: Vintage, 1970).

15. Moretti, *New Geography of Jobs*, 11.

16. Of course, as Alan Mallach points out in *The Divided City: Poverty and Prosperity in Urban America* (Washington, DC: Island Press, 2018), this wealth is not always spread equally, but policymakers in growing cities are better positioned to correct these inequities than in stagnant or declining cities.

17. Emily Badger, "Covid Didn't Kill Cities. Why Was That Prophecy So Alluring?" *New York Times*, July 12, 2021, https://www.nytimes.com/2021/07/12/upshot/covid-cities-predictions-wrong.html.

18. For a comprehensive treatment of the issue of US economic stagnation, the reader is encouraged to see Tyler Cowen, *The Great Stagnation: How America Ate All the Low-Hanging Fruit of Modern History, Got Sick, and*

Will (Eventually) Feel Better (Boston: Dutton, 2011). Real wage growth data from the Bureau of Labor Statistics. For more on the productivity slowdown, see Robert J. Godon, "Is U.S. Economic Growth Over? Faltering Innovation Confronts the Six Headwinds," NBER Working Paper Series (August 2012). For the decline in entrepreneurship, see Hugo Hopenhayn, Julian Neira, and Rish Singhania, "From Population Growth to Firm Demographics: Implications for Concentration, Entrepreneurship and the Labor Share," NBER Working Paper Series (December 2018). For declining mobility, see William H. Frey, "U.S. Migration Still at Historically Low Levels, Census Shows," Brookings Institution, November 20, 2017, https://www.brookings.edu/blog/the -avenue/2017/11/20/u-s-migration-still-at-historically-low-levels-census -shows/.

19. Granted, San Jose doesn't have Disney World!

20. All housing cost data drawn from Zillow (2021).

21. For an exceptional example, see Wilkerson, *Warmth of Other Suns*, on the Great Migration, in which millions of African Americans left rural, southern poverty for prosperous, northern industrial cities.

22. Not to mention cultural growth, which similarly benefits from agglomeration economies.

23. Chang-Tai Hsieh and Enrico Moretti, "Housing Constraints and Spatial Misallocation," *American Economic Journal: Macroeconomics* 11, no. 2 (April 2019).

24. Gilles Duranton and Diego Puga, "Urban Growth and Its Aggregate Implications," NBER Working Paper Series (December 2019), https:// www.nber.org/system/files/working_papers/w26591/w26591.pdf.

25. Peter Ganong and Daniel W. Shoag, "Why Has Regional Income Convergence in the U.S. Declined?" NBER Working Paper Series (July 2017), https://www.nber.org/papers/w23609.

26. For a robust defense of growth, see Tyler Cowen, *Stubborn Attachments: A Vision for a Society of Free, Prosperous, and Responsible Individuals* (San Francisco: Stripe Press, 2018).

CHAPTER 5: APARTHEID BY ANOTHER NAME

1. Larry Buchanan, Quotrung Bui, and Jugal K. Patel, "Black Lives Matter May Be the Largest Movement in U.S. History," *New York Times*, July 3, 2020, https://www.nytimes.com/interactive/2020/07/03/us/george -floyd-protests-crowd-size.html.

2. Jessica Trounstine, *Segregation by Design* (Cambridge: Cambridge University Press, 2018), 94.

3. As Rothstein, *Color of Law* notes, a majority of the committee that drafted the Standard Zoning Enabling Act, as well as many early zoning framers, were vocal segregationists.

4. Christopher Silver, "The Racial Origins of Zoning in American Cities," in *Urban Planning and the African American Community: In the Shadows*, edited by June Manning Thomas and Marsha Ritzdorf (Thousand Oaks, CA: Sage Publications, 1997).

5. Exceptions are often made for "servants' quarters" in single-family zones, a reflection of their classist origins. Such anachronistic language lingered in the zoning code of Fairfax County, Virginia, until 2019 and continues to survive in many ordinances.

6. In most major American cities, historically "Black neighborhoods" are more often than not located in flood zones or downwind of noxious industrial emissions. This is by design.

7. See Charles E. Connerly, *The Most Segregated City in America: City Planning and Civil Rights in Birmingham, 1920–1980* (Charlottesville: University of Virginia Press, 2005), for an extensive study of how planning perpetuated extreme segregation in Birmingham.

8. As Rothstein (*Color of Law*, 48) notes, race continues to play a major role in determinations regarding variances and rezonings.

9. This gave rise also to the phenomenon of redlining, discussed in detail in Rothstein, *Color of Law*.

10. Thomas C. Schelling, "Models of Segregation," *American Economic Review* 59, no. 2 (May 1969). As economist Thomas Schelling has observed, even small preferences for segregation will trend toward more segregated outcomes. Combining such small preferences with a

zoning policy dictated by risk-averse homeowners virtually guarantees segregation.

11. See Trounstine, *Segregation by Design*, 211.

12. See Wolf, *Zoning of America*.

13. See Trounstine, *Segregation by Design*.

14. While highly imperfect, the Mount Laurel doctrine is perhaps one of the best attempts by the courts to rectify zoning-induced segregation. New Jersey municipalities nonetheless retain wide latitude to write their own zoning ordinances, making enforcement of affordable obligations a game of whack-a-mole. For a simple explanation of how Mount Laurel works, see "Mount Laurel Doctrine," Fair Share Housing Center, https://fair sharehousing.org/mount-laurel-doctrine/.

15. Lisa Prevost, *Snob Zones: Fear, Prejudice, and Real Estate* (Boston: Beacon Press, 2015).

16. The prototypical exclusionary suburb, Darien has a median household income of $208,848 and is 90 percent White.

17. What does preserving character mean in the context of a town like Darien? Darien was once a "sundown" town, forbidding residence to all but Anglo-Saxon Protestants.

18. Douglas S. Massey and Zoltan L. Hahjnal, "The Changing Geographic Structure of Black-White Segregation in the United States," *Social Science Quarterly* 76, no. 3 (1995), https://psycnet.apa.org/record /1996-17009-001.

19. See Trounstine, *Segregation by Design* for a full study design.

20. Matthew Ressenger, "The Impact of Land Use Regulation on Racial Segregation: Evidence from Massachusetts Zoning Borders," working paper, November 26, 2013, https://scholar.harvard.edu/files/resseger/ files/resseger_jmp_11_25.pdf.

21. See Michael C. Lens and Paavo Monkkonen, "Do Strict Land Use Regulations Make Metropolitan Areas More Segregated by Income?" *Journal of the American Planning Association* 82, no. 1 (2016), https://www .tandfonline.com/doi/abs/10.1080/01944363.2015.1111163.

22. In Boston, for example, the life expectancy ranges from a high of ninety -two in the affluent, overwhelmingly White neighborhood of Back Bay to fifty-nine in the working-class, majority African American neighbor-hood of Roxbury. Aggressive zoning helps to underwrite this segregation.

23. Abigail Thernstrom and Stephan Thernstrom, "Black Progress: How Far We've Come, and How Far We Have to Go," Brookings Institution, March 1, 1998. The share of White respondents who say they would move if a Black family moved in next door fell from nearly 44 percent in the 1958 to *1 percent* in 1998; Tessa E. S. Charlesworth and Mahzarin R. Banaji, "Patterns of Implicit and Explicit Attitudes: I. Long-Term Change and Stability from 2007 to 2016," *Psychological Science* (January 2019), https://journals.sagepub.com/doi/abs/10.1177/0956797618813087/. This 2019 study found an especially marked decrease in racist attitudes between 2007 and 2016.

24. Ruth Igielnik, "70% of Americans Say U.S. Economic System Unfairly Favors the Powerful," Pew Research Center, January 9, 2020, https://www.pewresearch.org/fact-tank/2020/01/09/70-of-americans-say-u-s -economic-system-unfairly-favors-the-powerful/. Indeed, fears that "the system is rigged" now seem to be driving national politics.

25. "Poll: The Public Overwhelmingly Believes Affordability Should Be a Top National Priority; Expects Congress and President to Take Major Action," Opportunity Starts at Home, March 28, 2019, https://www .opportunityhome.org/pollpressrelease/. Housing affordability has recently emerged as a top issue for voters; Bryan Anderson, "Top Priority for California Voters Heading into 2020 Primary? Homelessness," *Sacramento Bee*, January 16, 2020, https://www.sacbee.com/news/politics -government/capitol-alert/article239325588.html. Housing insecurity is now acknowledged as the top issue in California.

CHAPTER 6: SPRAWL BY DESIGN

1. Especially New York City.
2. David Owen, *Green Metropolis: Why Living Smaller, Living Closer, and Driving Less Are the Keys to Sustainability* (New York: Riverhead Books, 2010).

3. James Howard Kunstler's *The Geography of Nowhere: The Rise and Decline of America's Man-Made Landscape* (New York: Free Press, 1994) is easily the most colorful of the many anti-sprawl manifestos.

4. See Charles Marohn, *Strong Towns: A Bottom-Up Revolution to Rebuild American Prosperity* (Hoboken, NJ: Wiley, 2019) for a thoroughgoing critique of sprawl from a fiscal perspective.

5. United States Census Bureau, "We Are Gathered Here," March 4, 2015, https://www.census.gov/library/visualizations/2015/comm/cb15-33 _gathered_here.html.

6. Jose M. Rey Benayas, "Rewilding: As Farmland and Villages Are Abandoned, Forests, Wolves, and Bears Are Returning to Europe," *The Conversation*, July 2, 2019, https://theconversation.com/rewilding-as-farm land-and-villages-are-abandoned-forests-wolves-and-bears-are-return ing-to-europe-119316. In Europe, where the phenomenon is known as "rewilding," the effects of this development can easily be seen from satellite imagery.

7. US Energy Information Administration, "Use of Energy Explained: Energy in Homes," June 2021, https://www.eia.gov/energyexplained/use -of-energy/homes.php.

8. US Energy Information Administration, "Apartments in Buildings with 5 or More Units Use Less Energy than Other Home Types," https:// www.eia.gov/todayinenergy/detail.php?id=11731#.

9. Robert Bruegmann, *Sprawl: A Compact History* (Chicago: University of Chicago Press, 2005).

10. Fishman, *Bourgeois Utopias*.

11. For a typical example, see City of New York Zoning Resolution Section 23-63.

12. For the environmental costs of yards, see Ellen Paul, "Lawns May Be Green, but They're Terrible for the Environment," *Greater Greater Washington*, June 20, 2019, https://ggwash.org/view/72499/lawns-are-good -for-almost-nothing-environment-eco-landscaping.

13. Eric Holthaus, "Lawns Are the No. 1 Irrigated 'Crop' in America. They Need to Die," Grist, May 2, 2019, https://grist.org/article/lawns-are -the-no-1-agricultural-crop-in-america-they-need-to-die/.

14. I now live in West Los Angeles, where I enjoy no such luxuries!

15. Owen, *Green Metropolis*.

16. Edward Glaeser and Matthew Kahn, "The Greenness of Cities: Carbon Dioxide Emissions and Urban Development," *Journal of Urban Economics* 67, no. 3 (May 2010), https://ideas.repec.org/a/eee/juecon/ v67y2010i3p404-418.html.

17. "Transit-Supportive Densities and Land Uses: A PSRC Guidance Paper," Puget Sound Regional Council, February 2015; Erick Guerra and Robert Cervero, "Transit and the 'D' Word," *Access Magazine* 40 (Spring 2012), https://www.accessmagazine.org/spring-2012/transit-d-word/.

18. Assume a standard five-thousand-square-foot minimum lot size and a standard fifty-foot-wide adjacent right-of-way.

19. Jonathan Levine, *Zoned Out: Regulation, Markets, and Choices in Transportation and Metropolitan Land Use* (Washington, DC: Resources for the Future, 2005).

20. Emily Hamilton and Eli Dourado, "The Premium for Walkable Development under Land Use Regulations," Mercatus Research Paper, February 13, 2018, https://www.mercatus.org/publications/urban-economics/ premium-walkable-development-under-land-use-regulations.

21. Consider again the example at the start of this chapter: the specific zoning request was to allow more than single-family homes *within a quarter mile of a major subway station*.

22. As we discuss in chapter 3, the cost increases associated with minimum parking requirements are also significant.

23. For household carbon emissions by city, see Glaeser and Kahn, "Greenness of Cities."

24. For household energy consumption by city, see "The Cities and States Using the Most and Least Residential Electricity," Cision PR Newswire, April 22, 2019, https://www.prnewswire.com/news-releases/the-cities-and -states-using-the-most-and-least-residential-electricity-300835369.html.

25. If you're curious, regions like the Northeast and the Midwest generally fall in between these extremes.

26. This is certainly true of Lexington, Kentucky, where I grew up.

CHAPTER 7: TOWARD A LESS BAD ZONING

1. Richard D. Kahlenberg, "How Minneapolis Ended Single-Family Zoning," Century Foundation, October 24, 2019, https://tcf.org/content/report/minneapolis-ended-single-family-zoning/.

2. For a national survey of ADU ordinances, see Salim Furth and Jess Remington, "Ordinances at Work: Seven Communities That Welcome Accessory Dwelling Units," Mercatus Center Policy Brief, April 2021, https://www.mercatus.org/publications/land-use-regulations/ordinances-work.

3. Robert Steuteville, "Gentle Density: Making Neighborhoods Transit-Readi," *Public Square*, August 8, 2018, https://www.cnu.org/public square/2018/08/30/gentle-density-making-neighborhoods-transit-ready.

4. For more on parking policy, see Shoup, *High Cost of Free Parking*.

5. Linda Poon, "Buffalo Becomes First City to Bid Minimum Parking Goodbye," *Bloomberg CityLab*, January 9, 2017, https://www.bloomberg .com/news/articles/2017-01-09/buffalo-is-the-first-to-abandon-mini mum-parking-requirements-citywide.

6. Zoe Jackson, "Minneapolis City Council Unanimously Eliminates Parking Requirements," *StarTribune*, May 14, 2021, https://www.star tribune.com/minneapolis-city-council-unanimously-eliminates-park ing-requirements/600057275/.

7. Return to chapter 3 for a deeper discussion of how minimum floor areas and lot sizes work.

8. Kim Norvell, "Des Moines Lowers Size Requirements for New Homes in Contentious Zoning Code," *Des Moines Register*, August 26, 2019, https://www.desmoinesregister.com/story/money/business/develop ment/2019/08/26/des-moines-development-zoning-code-minimum -square-footage-home-building-new-construction-housing/212062 2001/. Depending on the design of the home, Des Moines zoning may mandate that homes be as large as 1,700 square feet.

9. For a history of SROs, see Growth, *Living Downtown.*

10. For a history of mobile homes in America, see Allan D. Wallis, *Wheel Estate: The Rise and Decline of Mobile Homes* (Oxford: Oxford University Press, 1991).

11. Laurel Wamsley, "Oregon Legislature Votes to Essentially Ban Single-Family Zoning," NPR, July 1, 2019, https://www.npr.org/2019/07/01/737798440/oregon-legislature-votes-to-essentially-ban-single-family-zoning.

12. Dan Bertolet and Nisma Gabobe, "LA ADU Story: How a State Law Sent Granny Flats Off the Charts," Sightline Institute, April 5, 2019, https://www.sightline.org/2019/04/05/la-adu-story-how-a-state-law-sent-granny-flats-off-the-charts/.

13. "California ADU Growth by City from 2012–2019, Charted," Building an ADU, August 22, 2020, https://www.buildinganadu.com/adu-blog/california-adu-charts.

14. "California ADU Law Changes 2020," Action ADU, July 23, 2020, https://actonadu.com/blog/california-adu-law-changes-2020.

15. At the time of writing, the state has also recently passed SB 9, legalizing duplexes statewide.

16. Texas and Oklahoma passed similar bills in 2019 and 2020, respectively. See M. Nolan Gray, "What Can Policymakers Do about Surging Building Materials Costs?" Pacific Research Institute, August 10, 2021, pacificresearch.org/what-can-policymakers-do-about-surging-building-materials-costs/.

17. Tracy Jan, "Trump Gutted Obama-Era Housing Discrimination Rules. Biden's Bringing Them Back," *Washington Post*, April 13, 2021, https://www.washingtonpost.com/us-policy/2021/04/13/hud-biden-fair-housing-rules/.

18. Indeed, many of the critiques of zoning discussed in part II were well documented by the Douglas Commission over fifty years ago.

19. Jenny Schuetz, "HUD Can't Fix Exclusionary Zoning without CDBG Funds," Brookings Institution, October 15, 2018, https://www.brook

ings.edu/research/hud-cant-fix-exclusionary-zoning-by-withholding
-cdbg-funds/.

20. H.R. 2483—Build More Housing Near Homes Act of 2021 (117th Congress), https://www.congress.gov/bill/117th-congress/house-bill/2483/text?r=2&s=1.

21. See Hirt, *Zoned in the USA*, for a comparative survey of zoning.

22. For a detailed summary of how Japanese zoning works, see Japanese Ministry of Land, Infrastructure, and Transport, "Introduction of Urban Land Use Planning System in Japan," 2003, https://drive.google.com/file/d/1hzbhGNMp-P7lnp2-VXRjJVjDOAmNQqiO/view; the growing appreciation for Japanese zoning begins with this 2014 blog post by "Urban kchoze": http://urbankchoze.blogspot.com/2014/04/japanese-zoning.html.

23. Compare to the US, where flat zoning strictly prohibits such use mixture, a distinction we discussed back in chapter 2.

24. Robin Harding, "Why Tokyo Is the Land of Rising Home Construction but Not Prices," *Financial Times*, August 3, 2016, https://www.ft.com/content/023562e2-54a6-11e6-befd-2fc0c26b3c60.

CHAPTER 8: THE CASE FOR ABOLISHING ZONING

1. Consider housing production. Under normal conditions, a house might behave more like something that we consume rather than an investment. That is to say, we ought to approach housing like we approach a car or a laptop: you use it over a few years, it gradually falls in value, and you sell it for a fraction of what you paid for it—no windfall involved, except to the extent that the land itself has appreciated. In Japan, this is how housing works, with "used" housing making up a paltry 15 percent of the market, partly owing to the need to regularly rebuild in light of the country's regular earthquakes. By contrast, in the US, a full 90 percent of houses sold are used. Here in the US, we think of our homes as something we eventually plan to cash in on, an investment off of which we hope to eventually earn a tidy profit.

Why is the US so different? In part, because we heavily incentivize homeowners to view their house as an investment. Indeed, federal tax policy treats housing wealth better than most other types of investment, allowing you to deduct the interest on your mortgage, deduct up to $10,000 in local property taxes, and exempt up to half a million dollars in the profits you may make from selling your home from capital gains taxes. Many Americans have rationally responded to this set of incentives by plowing as much of their wealth into their homes as they can afford, with the hope of a big payoff down the road as housing costs presumably continue to rise. The trouble is that, in a housing market where the supply can rise to meet demand, housing prices may not follow an unending upward trajectory. Homeowning Americans, again responding to this clear set of incentives, will thus always have some motive to keep housing scarce as a way to increase the value of their largest investment.

2. The example of accessory dwelling unit (ADU) preemption in California is instructive in this regard: the push to allow additional housing units on lots with detached single-family houses didn't begin in 2020. On the contrary, the 2020 bills were mainly focused on beefing up the preemption package that passed in 2016. The 2016 reforms were themselves a follow-up to a 2002 bill, the first to require that every California municipality set up a ministerial process for approving ADUs. And the 2002 bill was *itself* a follow-up to a 1982 bill encouraging the adoption of ADU ordinances.

Why the constant need for follow-up? Because the municipalities that the repeated attempts at preemption had in mind for reform—affluent inner suburbs with a large inventory of low-density single-family homes near jobs and quality public services—either never adopted ADU ordinances or adopted them but found discrete zoning mechanisms for blocking new ADU construction, including through owner-occupancy requirements, unworkable setback rules, and onerous parking and massing requirements, resulting in few ADUs actually being built.

It seems like California's 2020 ADU preemption bills have finally ironed out all the kinks. But nearly forty years is an incredible amount of time to fix one small element of our broken zoning system, and across this time span, most other elements of California zoning grew exponentially more restrictive. Single-family zoning, after all, is only one policy on a long list of necessary changes to zoning. It should go without saying that half a century of state preemption whack-a-mole is not a sustainable path to zoning reform. It would take fundamental changes to our society—such as the forced consolidation of municipalities—to deal with this type of bad faith maneuvering around state and federal efforts to reform zoning. As with totally restructuring housing markets in the US, this is less likely to happen than outright zoning abolition.

Perhaps the best-case scenario for zoning reform would be for more states to implement an institution like New Jersey's Mount Laurel doctrine. The doctrine has gone through multiple iterations since 1975, when the New Jersey Supreme Court first struck down the use of zoning to exclude low-income households in *South Burlington County N.A.A.C.P. v. Mount Laurel Township*, but it generally works like this: Each municipality must adjust its zoning to allow its "fair share" of housing of various typologies to be built, with special attention paid to housing serving those of the least means. Where municipalities fail to meet this obligation, a developer may sue for changes to the zoning where the proposed development would bring a municipality closer to compliance.

In one sense, the Mount Laurel doctrine has been a major success, certainly if you grade along the curve of housing politics in the United States: since 1985, when the initial framework was first finalized, *Mount Laurel* has facilitated the construction of approximately sixty thousand below-market-rate units and helped in the construction of many more market-rate units. When combined with the New Jersey court system's active role in combating local zoning overreach, it has no doubt worked to keep the Garden State more affordable, more prosperous, less segregated, and less sprawling than it might otherwise have been.

But the history of *Mount Laurel* has been a history of fits and starts, with politics often intervening to lower allocation requirements or suspend the process altogether. Old pathologies continue to survive in this new system: Many affluent New Jersey suburbs persist in permitting as little new housing construction as the state courts will allow, often after years of litigation to minimize their housing obligations. Major employment centers like Princeton remain strikingly underbuilt, locking many New Jerseyans out of well-paying jobs and quality public services. Much of the housing that is allowed invariably takes a low-density, auto -oriented form, as is often still mandated by local zoning. The Mount Laurel doctrine is a dramatic improvement over the typical state land-use regulation regime, but we can—and must—do better.

3. This issue is hardly theoretical, as any practicing planner could tell you. In a recent case in Logan Circle, a neighborhood in Washington, DC, a popular beer garden opened up along a commercial strip adjacent to a residential neighborhood. The results were predictable: the beer garden was noisy and neighboring residents loudly complained, and yet zoning was oddly silent on the whole matter. By simplistically limiting its focus to shuffling broad uses into discrete districts, DC zoning largely ignored the issue of noise spilling over district boundaries and across neighborhoods, a major source of land-use conflict in cities. As a result, neighbors were forced to take the curious step of threatening the beer garden's liquor license as a way of forcing the business owner to the table; zoning, theoretically our system for separating incompatible uses, proved oddly aloof, as it so often does in such cases.

4. Indeed, the knowledge necessary to engage in this type of planning may take a form inaccessible to planners by its very nature. See Michael Polanyi, *The Tacit Dimension*, rev. ed. (Chicago: University of Chicago Press, 2009).

5. For more on this issue, see John William Reps, *Requiem for Zoning* (Ithaca, NY: Program in Urban and Regional Studies, Cornell University, 1964), 60.

6. F. A. Hayek, "The Use of Knowledge in Society," *American Economic Review* 35, no. 4, (September 1945), https://www.kysq.org/docs/ Hayek_45.pdf. Indeed, the epistemological critique leveled against comprehensive economic planning by the economist F. A. Hayek (1945) could be seamlessly applied to contemporary efforts at comprehensive land-use planning.

CHAPTER 9: THE GREAT UNZONED CITY

1. Adam McCann, "Most Diverse Cities in the U.S.," WalletHub, April 19, 2021, https://wallethub.com/edu/most-diverse-cities/12690.
2. This and all subsequent housing data from the US Census Bureau Permits Survey, via housingdata.app by Sid Kapur.
3. Nonetheless, zoning lost 14,142 to 6,555.
4. Salient concerns over the loss of property rights and the added risk of corruption—two zoning critiques that deserve more attention than they receive today—also helped to embolden the opposition.
5. Virginia Kelsey, Rives Taylor, Joe Douglas Webb, and Patrick Condon, "Zoning Houston: A Guide," *Cite*, Fall 1992–Winter 1993, http://offcite .org/wp-content/uploads/sites/3/2010/03/ZoningHouston_Kelsey TaylorWebbCondon_Cite29.pdf.
6. For a survey of the rise of deed restrictions and other forms of private land-use governance, see Robert H. Nelson, *Private Neighborhoods and the Transformation of Local Government* (Washington, DC: Urban Land Institute, 2005).
7. In any other city, enforcement of the provisions of a deed restriction is left to parties to its provisions.
8. M. Nolan Gray, "Are Houston's Deed Restrictions 'Basically Zoning'?" *Market Urbanism*, April 11, 2018, https://marketurbanism.com/2018 /04/11/houstons-deed-restrictions-basically-zoning. The following section reformulates ideas first advanced here, drawing heavily on Siegan, *Land Use without Zoning*, chapter 3.

9. The exact figure remains uncertain, but both Bernard Siegan, *Land Use without Zoning*, 2nd ed. (Lanham, MD: Rowman and Littlefield, 2020), and Teddy M. Kapur, "Land Use Regulation in Houston Contradicts the City's Free Market Reputation," ELR News and Analysis (2004) posit roughly a quarter.

10. M. Nolan Gray, "The Case for Subsidizing Deed Restrictions," *Market Urbanism*, May 9, 2018, https://marketurbanism.com/2018/05/09/case-subsidizing-deed-restrictions/. The following section draws heavily from this earlier blog post, which also draws heavily on Siegan, *Land Use without Zoning*.

11. Siegan, *Land Use without Zoning*.

12. We might put on some DJ Screw, for added effect.

13. Bertaud, *Order without Design*; inspired in turn by Hayek, "Use of Knowledge in Society."

14. Jane Jacobs, *The Death and Life of Great American Cities* (New York: Vintage, 1961).

15. Such an arrangement flips the script of zoning, forcing those with the more restrictive land-use preferences to partly shoulder the cost of their land-use preferences.

16. Houston Code of Ordinances, Chapter 30.

17. Houston Code of Ordinances, Chapter 10, Articles VIII and XI.

18. Houston Code of Ordinances, Chapter 21.

19. Houston Code of Ordinances Chapter 10, Article VIII, Sec. 10-272; Chapter 31, Article I, Sec. 10-272.

20. Houston Code of Ordinances Chapter 28, Article III, Section Sec. 28-124; Chapter 3, Article 1, Section 3-2.

21. Michael Lewyn, "How Overregulation Creates Sprawl (Even in a City without Zoning)," *Wayne Law Review* 50 (October 2005), https://papers.ssrn.com/sol3/papers.cfm?abstract_id=837244.

22. Houston Code of Ordinances, Chapter 26, Article VIII. These rules are reliably bizarre: for example, a "bar" must provide fourteen spaces per thousand square feet, while a "tavern" must provide ten.

23. Houston Code of Ordinances, Chapter 42, Article III, Division 8.

24. M. Nolan Gray, "How Car-Clogged Houston Could Be a Climate Policy Leader," *Bloomberg CityLab*, May 21, 2020, https://www.bloom berg.com/news/articles/2020-05-21/houston-s-climate-plan-could -make-it-a-green-model.

25. Nancy Sarnoff and Erin Mulvaney, "Talk of Ashby Tower and Houston's Lack of Zoning Keep Rising," *Houston Chronicle*, July 7, 2016, https://www.houstonchronicle.com/business/real-estate/looped-in/ article/Talk-of-Ashby-tower-and-Houston-s-lack-of-zoning-8347244 .php#photo-10478599.

26. For a detailed study of this, see M. Nolan Gray and Adam Millsap, "Subdividing the Unzoned City: An Analysis of the Causes and Effects of Houston's 1998 Subdivision Reform," *Journal of Planning Education and Research* (July 2020), https://journals.sagepub.com/doi/full /10.1177/0739456X20935156.

27. Houston didn't even need these added safeguards to reject zoning: the 1993 election occurred in a low-turnout odd year, with a simple majority rejecting. But given the impact zoning can have on a city, such provisions should be added to avoid special interests hammering through its adoption.

28. For other Texas cities that held ill-fated zoning referenda, see Siegan, *Land Use without Zoning*.

29. As with Houston's minimum lot size opt-out provisions, these rules should automatically sunset after a specified period—say, thirty years— absent renewal via supermajority approval.

30. Preemption energies currently dedicated to addressing the symptoms of zoning might usefully be shifted to this more ambitious program, especially in growing states where newly incorporated municipalities might feel the temptation to adopt zoning.

31. For more on the recurring history of Houston flooding, see Phillip W. Magness, "Houston Flooding in Historical Perspective: No, Zoning Would Not Have Stopped Harvey," 2017, https://philmagness.com

/2017/08/houston-in-historical-perspective-no-zoning-would-not-have
-stopped-harvey/.

32. M. Nolan Gray, "Houston's Zoning Wasn't the Problem," *Bloomberg CityLab*, September 4, 2017, https://www.bloomberg.com/news/articles /2017-09-04/how-houston-s-zoning-can-help-hurricane-harvey-recovery.

33. To their great credit, the current generation of Houston planners are busy undertaking many of the ideas discussed in the next chapter: the city is making major investments in transit, has adopted ambitious bicycle and open space plans, and is working to establish what could soon be the largest land bank in the nation.

CHAPTER 10: PLANNING AFTER ZONING

1. Thomas Campanella, "Jane Jacobs and the Death and Life of American Planning," *Places Journal* (April 2011), https://placesjournal.org/ article/jane-jacobs-and-the-death-and-life-of-american-planning/?cn-re loaded=1.

2. The author speaks from experience.

3. Hiral Jariwala, "Noise Pollution & Human Health: A Review," conference paper, March 2017, https://www.researchgate.net/profile/Hiral -Jariwala/publication/319329633_Noise_Pollution_Human_Health _A_Review/links/59a54434a6fdcc773a3b1c49/Noise-Pollution -Human-Health-A-Review.pdf.

4. WHO European Centre for Environment and Health, "Burden of Disease from Environmental Noise: Qualification of Healthy Life Years Lost in Europe," 2011, https://www.euro.who.int/__data/assets/pdf_file /0008/136466/e94888.pdf.

5. Tracy K. Swinburn, Monica S. Hammer, and Richard L. Neitzel, "Valuing Quiet: An Economic Assessment of US Environmental Noise as a Cardiovascular Health Hazard," *American Journal of Preventative Medicine* 49, no. 3, https://www.ncbi.nlm.nih.gov/pmc/articles/PMC4819987/.

6. Lexingon-Fayette Urban County Government, "Code of Ordinances," Sec. 14-72.

7. Planners should look to and learn from earlier efforts at performance zoning, which attempted to replace zoning with performance standards in a similar kind of way. See Kendig, *Performance Zoning*.

8. Stephen Menendian and Samir Gambhir, "The Roots of Structural Racism Project: Twenty-First Century Racial Residential Segregation in the United States," Othering & Belonging Institute, June 30, 2021, https://belonging.berkeley.edu/roots-structural-racism.

9. Richard Fry and Paul Taylor, "The Rise of Residential Segregation by Income," Pew Research Center, August 1, 2012, https://www.pew research.org/social-trends/2012/08/01/the-rise-of-residential-seg regation-by-income/.

10. Indeed, they have a legal obligation to do so, pursuant to the Fair Housing Act's Affirmatively Furthering Fair Housing provisions.

11. John Eligon, Yamiche Alcindor, and Agustin Armendariz, "Program to Spur Low-Income Housing Is Keeping Cities Segregated," *New York Times*, July 2, 2017, https://www.nytimes.com/2017/07/02/us/federal -housing-assistance-urban-racial-divides.html.

12. This is different from the previously discussed Mount Laurel program, in which the state actually undertakes the Rube Goldbergian task of allocating how much housing each municipality must build over a specified period; under the Chapter 40B program, if income-restricted units don't account for 10 percent of the stock in any given municipality, its provisions are automatically triggered.

13. Quentin Brummet and David Reed, "The Effects of Gentrification on the Well-Being and Opportunity of Original Resident Adults and Children," United States Census Bureau, July 2019, https://www.census .gov/library/working-papers/2019/adrm/data-linkage-gentrification -effects.html.

14. Emily Hamilton, "Inclusionary Zoning Hurts More Than It Helps," Mercatus Center Policy Brief, September 2019, https://www.mercatus.org/ publications/urban-economics/inclusionary-zoning-hurts-more-it-helps.

15. See, for example, Joe Cortright's plan for earmarking tax increment funds (TIF) for new income-restricted housing production. Joe Cortright,

"A Solution for Displacement: TIF for Affordable Housing," City Observatory, November 6, 2019, https://cityobservatory.org/a-solution -for-displacement-tif-for-affordable-housing/.

16. Yichen Su, "Gentrification Transforming Neighborhoods in Big Texas Cities," Federal Reserve Bank of Dallas, Fourth Quarter 2019, https:// www.dallasfed.org/research/swe/2019/swe1904/swe1904b.

17. Megan Kimble, "Building Trust," *Texas Observer*, April 6, 2020, https:// www.texasobserver.org/community-land-trust-texas/.

18. Gerard Koeppel, *City on a Grid: How New York Became New York* (Boston: De Capo Press, 2015).

19. Robert Steuteville, "Texas City Adopts Street Grid and Code," *Public Square*, November 15, 2019, https://www.cnu.org/publicsquare/2019 /11/15/texas-city-adopts-street-grid-and-code.

20. Bertaud, *Order without Design*, chap. 8.

APPENDIX: WHAT ZONING ISN'T

1. Kahlenberg, "How Minneapolis Ended Single-Family Zoning," offers a helpful explanation for Minneapolis's unprecedented reform.

2. See Badger and Bui, "Cities Start to Question an American Ideal" for instructive illustrations of this phenomenon.

3. This antiquated zoning has sparked a kind of regulatory whack-a-mole, in which New York City planners have been tasked with making sure that nothing *other* than manufacturing can be built in these zones.

4. For an extensive study of this in the context of unzoned Houston, see Siegan, *Land Use without Zoning*. We also cover this topic in chapter 9.

5. See Bertaud, *Order without Design*.

6. The curious reader should search online for the International Building Code.

7. While outside the scope of this book, it is important to note that excessively strict building codes can occasionally drive up housing costs.

8. For a deeper survey of subdivision regulations, refer to Eran Ben-Jopseph, "Facing Subdivision Regulations," in *Regulating Place: Standards and the Shaping of Urban America*, edited by Eran Ben-Joseph and Terry S. Szold (London: Routledge, 2004).

9. See *Penn Central Transportation Co. v. New York City* 438 U.S. 104 (1978).

10. Payton Chung, "DC Has More Historic Buildings than Boston, Chicago and Philadelphia Combined. Why?" *Greater Greater Washington*, August 3, 2020, https://ggwash.org/view/78627/dc-has-more-historic-buildings -than-boston-chicago-and-philadelphia-combined-why-2.

11. For a deep dive into California's dysfunctional environmental review system, see M. Nolan Gray, "How Californians Are Weaponing Environmental Law," *Atlantic*, March 12, 2021, https://www.theatlantic.com/ideas /archive/2021/03/signature-environmental-law-hurts-housing/618264/.

12. For more on this, see Bernard J. Frieden, *The Environmental Protection Hustle* (Cambridge, MA: MIT Press, 1979).

13. This term was originally coined by Fred P. Bosselman and David L. Callies, "The Quiet Revolution in Land Use Control," Council on Environmental Quality, 1971, which provides more background on the phenomenon.

14. For more on the "double veto," see Frank Popper, "Understanding American Land Use Planning since 1970," *Journal of American Planning Association* 54 (Summer 1988).

15. See Metro, "Urban Growth Boundary," February 24, 2020, https://www .oregonmetro.gov/urban-growth-boundary, for an accessible summary of Oregon's urban growth boundary policy.

16. For the full report, see New York City Department of City Planning, "Zoning for Coastal Flood Resiliency," May 2019, https://www1.nyc .gov/assets/planning/download/pdf/plans-studies/flood-resiliency-up date/zoning-for-coastal-flood-resiliency-info-brief.pdf.

17. For a list of the dozens of plans in effect in "unplanned" Houston, see City of Houston Planning and Development Department, "Houston General Plan," 2015, http://www.houstontx.gov/planhouston/index.html.

18. For a good example of a comprehensive plan, check out Lexington-Fayette Urban County Government Division of Planning, "Imagine Lexington," 2018.

19. These framers and their vision were discussed in chapter 1.

Recommended Reading

CHAPTER 1: WHERE ZONING COMES FROM

- For a broad history of cities in the US and the gradual evolution of institutions like zoning, see *Crabgrass Frontier* by Kenneth T. Jackson (Oxford University Press, 1987).
- For an in-depth history leading up to New York City's 1916 zoning ordinance, check out *Zoned American* by Seymour Toll (Grossman Publishers, 1969).
- For a legal history of early zoning up through and after *Euclid v. Ambler*, check out *The Zoning of America* by Michael Allan Wolf (University Press of Kansas, 2008).

CHAPTER 2: HOW ZONING WORKS

- For a more detailed explanation of how US zoning works—and how it differs from nearly every other system—check out *Zoned in the USA* by Sonia Hirt (Cornell University Press, 2014).
- For an accessible explanation of zoning, written for practicing developers and investors, check out *The Complete Guide to Zoning* by Dwight H. Merriam (McGraw-Hill, 2005).

- For an excellent survey of the economics of zoning, check out *Zoning Rules!* by William A. Fischel (Lincoln Institute of Land Policy, 2015).

CHAPTER 3: PLANNING AN AFFORDABILITY CRISIS

- For an early exploration of the contemporary housing affordability crisis, see *The Rent Is Too Damn High* by Matthew Yglesias (Simon and Schuster, 2012, digital only).
- For a detailed study of the "how and why" behind zoning delays, see *Neighborhood Defenders* by Katherine Levine Einstein, David Glick, and Maxwell Palmer (Cambridge University Press, 2019).
- For more on the high cost of certain zoning rules, see *The High Cost of Free Parking* by Donald Shoup (Routledge, 2011).

CHAPTER 4: THE WEALTH WE LOST

- For an early study of how artificial constraints on housing in wealthy cities are driving economic stagnation, see *The Gated City* by Ryan Avent (Kindle Single, 2011).
- For a broad look at the economic importance of dense cities and the zoning regulations holding them back, see *Triumph of the City* by Edward Glaeser (Penguin Press, 2011).
- For a more recent overview of the distressing economic implications of zoning, see *The New Geography of Jobs* by Enrico Moretti (Houghton Mifflin Harcourt, 2012).

CHAPTER 5: APARTHEID BY ANOTHER NAME

- For the best single book on how planners systematically segregated the United States by race, see *The Color of Law* by Richard Rothstein (Liveright, 2017).
- For a deeper dive into the relationship between zoning and segregation, including how segregation in turn shapes society, see *Segregation by Design* by Jessica Trounstine (Cambridge University Press, 2018).

- For a qualitative study of how zoning continues to perpetuate segregation in places like New England, see *Snob Zones* by Lisa Prevost (Beacon Press, 2015).

CHAPTER 6: SPRAWL BY DESIGN

- For an environmental defense of cities, *Green Metropolis* by David Owen is without a doubt the essential text (Riverhead Books, 2009).
- On the flip side, *The Environmental Protection Hustle* by Bernard J. Frieden examines the misuse of environmental rhetoric to thwart the growth of cities (MIT Press, 1979, out of print).
- In *Zoned Out*, Jonathan Levine examines how land-use regulation thwarts walkable and transit-oriented development, against clear market signals (RFF Press, 2005).

CHAPTER 7: TOWARD A LESS BAD ZONING

- For a great survey of the early YIMBY movement—the spark of the current housing reform moment—see *Golden Gates* by Conor Dougherty (Penguin Press, 2020).
- For a useful set of reforms to the substance and process of zoning, see *A Better Way to Zone* by Donald L. Elliott (Island Press, 2008).
- For a delightfully detailed dive into how cities can reform zoning and advance housing affordability, see *The Affordable City* by Shane Phillips (Island Press, 2020).

CHAPTER 8: THE CASE FOR ABOLISHING ZONING

- For the messy reality of how zoning ordinances emerge and evolve, see *The Politics of Zoning* by Stanislaw J. Makielski Jr. (Columbia University Press, 1966).
- For a fun romp through the day-to-day application of zoning as it exists in the real world, check out *The Zoning Game* by Richard Babcock (Lincoln Institute of Land Policy, 1966).

- To learn more about "local knowledge problems" that undermine zoning, see *The Death and Life of the Great American City* by Jane Jacobs (Vintage Books, 1961).

CHAPTER 9: THE GREAT UNZONED CITY

- For a landmark study of how non-zoning works in Houston, see *Land Use without Zoning* by Bernard H. Siegan (First published in 1961 by Random House. New edition released in 2020 with a foreword by the author).
- For a deep dive into how informal social norms work to settle disputes among neighbors, see *Order without Law* by Robert Ellickson (Harvard University Press, 1991).
- For a study of the rise of private forms of land-use regulation, see *Private Neighborhoods and the Transformation of Local Government* by Robert Nelson (Urban Land Institute, 2005).

CHAPTER 10: PLANNING AFTER ZONING

- For an exploration into how cities naturally design themselves and the role of planners, check out *Order without Design* by Alain Bertaud (MIT Press, 2018).
- For an explanation of the design standards that define modern cities, see *Streets and the Shaping of Towns and Cities* by Michael Southworth and Eran Ben-Joseph (McGraw-Hill, 1996).

APPENDIX: WHAT ZONING ISN'T

- For a survey of the economic forces that shape cities, see *Lectures on Urban Economics* by Jan K. Brueckner (MIT Press, 2011).
- For an overview of the broader planning landscape, check out *The Citizen's Guide to Planning* by Christopher Duerksen, Gregory Dale, and Donald Elliott (Routledge, 2009).

Index

Pages featuring photographs, maps, and drawings are shown in *italics*.

About the Author

M. Nolan Gray is a professional city planner with experience working on the front lines of zoning policy in New York City. He is an affiliated scholar with the Mercatus Center at George Mason University, where he helps to inform state and local policymakers on land-use regulation. Gray is currently completing a PhD in urban planning at the University of California, Los Angeles, where he serves on the board of the North Westwood Neighborhood Council.

In addition to this professional planning work, Gray is also a widely published writer on cities and a regular contributor to the popular blog *Market Urbanism*. His work has appeared in various outlets, including *Bloomberg CityLab*, the *Atlantic*, and *Forbes*. In addition to this written media, Gray regularly appears on national and local radio, podcasts, and television to discuss city planning issues. He is also the host of a new YouTube series, *Pop Culture Urbanism*.